Upper Fal

IN OLD PHOTOGRAPHS

There has been an inn on the site of the Lemon Arms in Mylor Bridge since at least 1765, when it was called the Griffin Inn. At this time it was used by the Carclew landlords to hold the Manor Court, where rents were paid and other business transacted on quarter days, after which the tenants were entertained to 'a glass of ale and a cut of roast beef'. In these early days the inn stood farther back from the road. It is likely that it had been enlarged by 1829, when it was known as the Red Lion and used by the Overseers of the Poor to hold meetings of the Vestry, a body that dealt with the business of the Poor House, which stood on the opposite side of the road (see p. 31). Records show that by 1837 the inn had become the Lemon Arms and that in the early twentieth century it was still used for the Manor Court as this picture shows, with tenants waiting outside before paying their rent. The lane on the far side of the inn, now known as New Row, was at one time called Navy Row as it was the home of several of the personnel of HMS *Ganges* (see pp. 14 & 15). The houses on the far side of the lane were destroyed by a German bomb in the early 1940s and the site is now the Lemon Arms car park. Near to the large tree above this row of houses the leat for the mill passes under the road on its way to Mill Quay. On the opposite side of the road was a saw-pit, near the present-day butchers. The Lemon Arms' stables and garden were farther down the road on the left which led to Mill Quay, near the site of the present post office. In the distance on the left stands the village smithy, where horses were shod and iron tyres fitted to wooden cartwheels on the banding-plate, which is still to be seen despite the recent demolition of this part of the village's heritage. Just off the picture to the right is one of several village pumps (mains water was only brought to Mylor in the 1950s) once used by the landlords for brewing beer and by the men of the village, who found its proximity to the Lemon Arms a great advantage.

Upper Fal

IN OLD PHOTOGRAPHS

PETER GILSON

Alan Sutton Publishing Limited
Phoenix Mill · Far Thrupp · Stroud
Gloucestershire

First Published 1994

Copyright © Peter Gilson, 1994

British Library Cataloguing in Publication Data.
A catalogue record for this book is available from
the British Library.

ISBN 0-7509-0392-9

Typeset in 9/10 Sabon.
Typesetting and origination by
Alan Sutton Publishing Limited.
Printed in Great Britain by
Redwood Books, Trowbridge.

This is a view of the western end of Devoran, looking across Restronguet Creek from the Carclew Deer Park. From nothing in 1880, the port of Devoran had grown up by 1840 mainly as a result of the completion of the Redruth and Chasewater Railway, connecting the port with all the mines between the Creek and Redruth. This is dealt with in greater detail on pp. 45–9.

Contents

The Fal Estuary: map drawn by Baptista Boazio in 1597.

Introduction

The magnificent tidal estuary of the River Fal and its tributaries penetrates 9 miles inland from Black Rock at its entrance. For centuries it has been used by seafarers for shelter and trade, and by the people living around its shores for subsistence farming and fishing, as well as for communications. At the head of almost every creek, at the point at which its stream has been bridged at the upper tidal limit, a settlement has grown up. In the past this location usually developed into a significant trading point because water transport was more significant up ·to the second decade of the twentieth century. A combination of these factors gave the estuary a character that persisted up to the mid-twentieth century, but this has been changed by the impact of modern society: improved road access has turned most villages into 'dormitory' settlements and the growing popularity of pleasure sailing has added to the problems brought about by the increasing number of holiday homes in the villages around the shores. But here we are concerned with the past. The photographs collected for this, the third volume in the trilogy of the Fal Estuary, are meant to afford the reader glimpses of past life, events that are now long over and places that have changed, sometimes beyond recognition.

Baptista Boazio's wonderful map (see pp. 6 & 7) shows the estuary as it used to be and is remarkable for the accuracy of its cartography, considering that the area was surveyed and the map drawn four centuries ago. After the written word, maps are the next best way in which we can compare conditions in the past with those of today. This map makes this possible. Tidal water penetrated much farther inland in 1597, with Tregony, Bissoe and Tresillian accessible. Villages exist today of which the map shows no trace – Devoran, Mylor, Flushing and Malpas – while settlements shown on the map have disappeared, and though Penryn, Truro and Tregony are shown as substantial towns, of Falmouth there is no sign – only Arwenack and Pendennis Castle existed four hundred years ago.

Pictorial evidence of the past spans an even shorter period: engravings and paintings were produced, but their accuracy is always in question. Photography came to Cornwall earlier than in many other places because of the scientific work and exhibitions of the Falmouth-based Royal Cornwall Polytechnic Society in its formative years. After 1840 not only was Robert Hunt experimenting here with early types of photography, especially 'daguerrotype' in Falmouth, but another photography pioneer, Fox Talbot, a nephew by marriage to Sir Charles Lemon (see pp. 36–7), was producing family photographs at Carclew, some of which date back to 1841. Photographers, both amateur and professional, were encouraged to exhibit their work at the annual 'Polytechnic' exhibition and Cornish people were among the first to see pictures and portraits produced by this new method. It is a pity that so few of them seem to exist today.

SECTION ONE

Carrick Roads

This three-masted sailing vessel is entering the harbour on the Pendennis side of Black Rock, under tow by one of the port's early tugs while another attendant vessel follows closely astern. This may have been a boarding steamer such as the *Alert*, which was mentioned in the *West Briton* of 29 March 1875: 'For many years it has been the custom of the ship-chandlers, outfitters and others to carry on a large trade afloat, vessels bound for the port being met outside the harbour.' *Alert* was built at the Sara and Burgess Foundry in Penryn for the chandlers J.H. Pope and Company.

This view of Carrick Roads from Pendennis headland, above the docks, shows ten large square-riggers at anchor waiting for orders. Before the invention of radio, ships at sea were virtually lost until the shores of Britain came into sight. They came close inshore off Lizard Point to be identified at the Lizard Signal Station, built originally by Fox's of Falmouth in 1872, then proceeded into Falmouth so that the captain could contact the ship's agent to find out where the owners of the cargo wanted to take delivery. Thus many ships left overseas ports with the simple instructions that they should proceed to 'Falmouth for orders'. Local newspapers regularly reported the shipping situation in the port. In October 1847 'about 200 sail chiefly corn-laden, some as large as 1200 tons, were at anchor in the harbour', while forty years later there had arrived 'in three days, 45 vessels for orders, totalling 32,374 tons'. In the latter case the average tonnage was only 719 tons, indicating that most of the arrivals were quite small. The appearance of the very large iron-hulled square-riggers associated with the port, such as *Herzogin Cecile*, *Lawhill*, *Pamir* and *Passat*, came only after 1880, carrying cargoes of non-perishable imports such as coal, wheat, timber and guano. This last commodity, made up of bird droppings found in vast deposits along the coast of Chile and Peru, was normally used as fertilizer. In April 1873, however, a somewhat unorthodox use for the cargo was reported when *Northumbria* arrived with the body of the master and part-owner, who had died in Peru, 'buried three feet deep in guano and in perfect condition when sent to St Ives for burial'.

Sweet May was one of the many sailing vessels, locally called 'barges', that carried a variety of cargoes into the many creeks of the Fal Estuary. 'Inside' barges, such as this, had no deck and plied only inside the estuary, at times dredging sand but also carrying cargo from larger ships at anchor in the harbour. Some were specialist barges such as those used by Carne's Brewery in Falmouth to take beer to Truro. 'Outside' barges, which sailed up to 50 miles in the open sea, were decked vessels and carried coal, building materials, sea sand, limestone and roadstone from the Lizard quarries. The limestone was taken to one of the many lime-kilns on the shores of the estuary. Roadstone was carried in this way up to the late 1940s.

Falmouth Quay Punts, such as *ICU*, seen here racing in a regatta in about 1895, were used to service larger sailing vessels coming to the port. Usually family-run boats, they would go 'out seeking' beyond the Lizard to contact a ship, which the punt would then serve throughout its stay in Falmouth. Conditions on board, with a large open cockpit and a simple coal-burning stove for cooking, were not ideal for a long period at sea. The main mast on these work boats was made short so that the yards and braces would not be fouled on coming alongside a square-rigger.

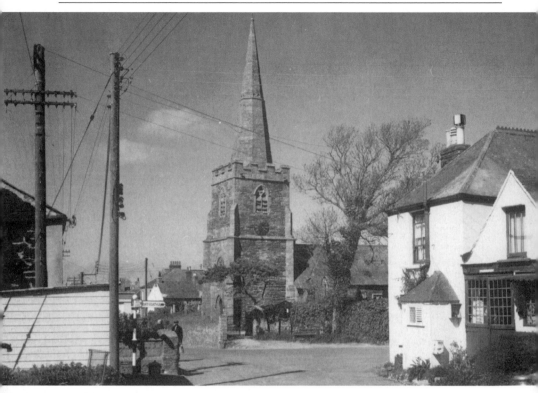

The peninsula forming the eastern shore of Falmouth Harbour is known as the Roseland but, as John Norden, map maker, observed in 1584, it 'has nothing to do with flowers, being derived from "rhos", the Celtic word for heath or gorse'. Over the four centuries since then much reclamation has taken place to turn the whole of this beautiful promontory – sea-girt on the east and deeply penetrated by creeks of the Fal on the west – into one of Cornwall's most productive agricultural areas. Its farming is mixed, although it is renowned for the quality of its livestock, and draught oxen were used up to the late nineteenth century. Growing cereals, hops and root crops, its high fertility was maintained by liberal use of seaweed, sand, pilchards (during a glut) and the produce of several limekilns on the shores of its western creeks. Gerrans, its only large settlement, is pictured here. Its spired church, prominently visible from most of the Roseland, dates from 1262, although it was rebuilt in 1849–50 and its spire was restored in 1890 at a cost of £102. *Kelly's Directory* of 1893 lists twenty-two farmers in the parish and the main landowners as Francis Gilbert Enys, HRH the Prince of Wales and the Ecclesiastic Commissioners.

Inside the beautiful St Just Creek stands one of the estuary's eight early churches, all of which are within 100 yards of tidal water. Only a visit to this place, preferably at high tide, can do justice to the church and its park-like graveyard. The remoteness of this area – one of its greatest attractions today – was exploited in the past. It was used as the 'Lazaretto' or quarantine station for the whole estuary, described in *Cooke's Cornwall* in 1830 as 'an old vessel lying aground on the south east shore and a little outside . . . where vessels perform quarantine'. The shores of the estuary were formerly more densely wooded than today and the timber was used for many purposes, including fuel, fencing, hurdle making and for charcoal burning, as advertised in the *West Briton* in March 1850: 'For Sale: Commerans Wood: a quantity of wood, cut and prepared for charcoal burning.'

HMS *Ganges* was for a time unique in the Royal Navy. All 'wooden walls' built in Britain were constructed of oak but, as each large ship of the line required the felling of about nine hundred trees, it was not surprising that supplies were running out. This ship was built in Bombay of teak and, launched in 1821, incorporated several innovative features based on French design which was reputedly superior to that in the RN. *Ganges* fulfilled different peacetime roles, including those of flagship and survey vessel, before returning to Britain for retirement in 1861, the same year that HMS *Warrior* came into service as the first British naval warship to be built entirely of iron. After four years of idleness, *Ganges* was sailed to Devonport, stripped of its armament and converted for use as a training ship for boys. On 30 January 1866 it arrived in Carrick Roads to be anchored in St Just Pool while the supporting shore facilities were established at the former RN dockyard at Mylor (see also *Falmouth*, p. 24 & *Lower Fal*, p. 124). In 1887–8 a complete overhaul was carried out in Devonport and fears were expressed that 'should *Ganges* once leave Falmouth she will never return . . . should this be true it will be a great loss to the port', but the ship returned in May 1888, having had its timbers inspected and bottom scraped, and having been thoroughly refitted. The return under tow from the tug *Valorous* is shown above, with St Mawes Castle and an

anchored square-rigger in the background. Many of the four hundred boys under training came from large, poor families unable to feed and clothe them adequately, or from the Union workhouses, so as to relieve the ratepayers of the cost of their upkeep. Below opposite is the starboard watch, posing with officers and instructors, probably on the exercise field behind the Mylor shore base. During their stay in the harbour the crew of the *Ganges* fulfilled many roles. They acted as fire-fighters (see *Falmouth*, p. 42), were entrants in local regattas and opponents in football matches, and the ship's band attended several social functions. One of the ship's most unusual operations was reported in June 1871, when 'a fine, full-rigged ship named the *Perseverance*, of 1197 tons, from Oran for Newcastle with a cargo of grass and lead, was towed into Falmouth harbour, her cargo being on fire. It had ignited whilst she was off the Lizard the previous day. The *Perseverance* was anchored in St Just Pool, near HMS *Ganges*. Pumps from the shore were immediately engaged by Messrs Broad and Sons, the agents for the ship, and the men and engines of the *Ganges* were quickly on board. For the whole of the day the cargo continued smouldering, at times emitting a flame. . . . the conflagration could not be kept under. As soon as the vessel was anchored it was thought desirable to scuttle her and the guns of the *Ganges* were brought to bear on her but owing to the compressed state of the cargo, the hull did not sink until five o'clock in the afternoon.' *Ganges*' eventual departure from Falmouth is seen pictured above and was reported in the *Falmouth and Penryn Times* of 28 August 1899: 'The most recent of Falmouth calamities – the removal of the famous training ship *Ganges* to Harwich – took place on Tuesday morning. She left her moorings at 10.45 in the morning and was taken in tow by the Government tug *Escort*, another tug taking up position at the stern. There was a heavy rain falling as the good old ship passed slowly out of the harbour, but there were large crowds of people who watched with melancholy interest her passage from our port where she had been such a familiar figure since 1865. Passing out of the harbour she dipped her flag as a token of farewell and the flag at Pendennis Castle was dipped in response.'

Apart from those times when they can be picked up from the shore at a low spring tide, the method of raising oysters entails dragging a heavily weighted 3 ft dredge along the sea floor for a distance, raising it and removing the oysters that are too large to pass through a standard ring, 2⅝ in. in diameter, as left. On the shallow edges of the banks in Carrick Roads, and the narrow upper part of the estuary between Turnaware and Malpas, the 'haul and tow' method is used, as below. A punt (rowing-boat) has two winches in the bow, one with a headline over the bow attached to an anchor and the other attached to the dredge over the stern. Dredging takes place by putting down the anchor and rowing stern-first to the limit of the headline; then the dredge is thrown over the stern and the punt moved forward using the headline winch, stopping at intervals to raise the dredge. In 1897 it was reported that, using this method, at Tolverne Reach, 'a hundred dredges were working, obtaining about 3000 per boat'. In two days it was estimated that three quarters of a million oysters were taken. The fishery provided a livelihood for many families in the Kea and Feock districts, where the

plum harvest had been a complete failure that year. In the deeper, more open waters of Carrick Roads gaff-rigged sailing boats, known locally as Falmouth Working Boats, are used. These vessels drift with the wind and tide, stopping at intervals to lift up to four dredges, one at a time. At the end of each drift the sails are hoisted and the boat taken back to start another drift. The picture above (reproduced by kind permission of Andrew Campbell) shows Frank Cock, the grand old man of the estuary, accompanied by a friendly seagull on *Morning Star*. This boat was 168 years old when mysteriously sunk at her moorings in Restronguet Creek in 1980. Its rejuvenated remains may still be seen as an exhibit in the Land's End leisure complex. In as early as 1602 the oyster fishery here was described by Richard Carew (a Cornish author and historian), who made it clear that oysters provided the food for all classes of society. Carrick Roads and many of the upper creeks supported the fishery as a staple food of the people. It seems to have been a largely domestic operation until the early years of the nineteenth century, when a series of severe winters on the east coast threatened the livelihood of the Kent and Essex oystermen who brought their stocks down and laid them in the Fal and Helford rivers (see *Lower Fal*, p. 155).

Towards the end of the nineteenth century, in an attempt to improve and regularize the oyster harvest, Cornwall County Council proposed to establish a County Fisheries School. The Royal Cornwall Polytechnic Society sought to have it based in Falmouth and undertook to organize its activities if partly subsidized by the Council. For the decade beginning in 1895 hatching took place in the Bar Pool, and 'spat' (oyster spawn) was laid on ceramic tiles in various parts of the estuary. These pictures of 1899 show the experiments in progress in Tolverne Reach. Unfortunately the lack of conspicuous success led to the withdrawal of the county grant and in 1902, in a terse report, the Polytechnic Society announced its regret at the termination of the experiments.

EMIGRATION   EMIGRATION

FOR QUEBEC,

THE SPLENDID

BARQUE

PARAGON

BURTHEN 600 TONS,

THOMAS DUNSTONE, Commander,

BRITISH BUILT, NEWLY COPPERED, AND THOROUGHLY REPAIRED,

Now lying at anchor at Malpas,

IN THIS PORT, AND WILL POSITIVELY SAIL

FOR QUEBEC,

WIND AND WEATHER PERMITTING, THE

FIRST WEEK IN NEXT MONTH, APRIL;

Presenting a superior opportunity to Cabin and Steerage Passengers intending to Emigrate to the Canadas, or to the United States,—as the accommodations for both are of a description seldom to be met with in Vessels employed in the Trade with North America.

EARLY APPLICATIONS SHOULD BE MADE AT THE OFFICE OF

Messrs. R. MICHELL & SON,

TRURO, OR TO THE CAPTAIN ON BOARD.

Dated Truro, March 2, 1847.

Over the last two centuries, mainly for economic reasons, many Cornish people have left the county for a new life overseas and many have embarked from the Fal. This poster is typical of many that encouraged miners and, to a lesser extent, agricultural workers to escape the nineteenth-century depression in mining and farming by emigrating, mainly to North America and the Antipodes. Many books have been written about the impact of Cornish emigration and in several continents the Cornish connection is still proudly remembered.

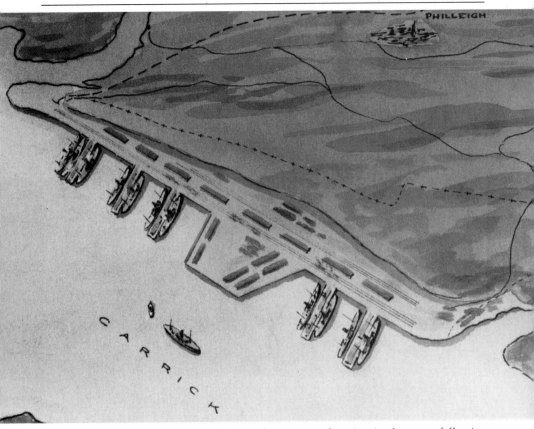

Ever since Falmouth Docks were built in their present location in the years following 1860, some experts have said that they had been built in the wrong place. Much of the costly dredging necessary in making the docks accessible to the increasingly large ocean-going vessels could have been saved, it has been argued, if wharves had been constructed nearer the deep channel running roughly north to south through Carrick Roads, but curving noticeably east in a wide meander towards the St Just shore. On the eastern side of the estuary, between Turnaware and St Just Creek, is, supposedly, the ideal spot, as this section of a painting of one of the schemes portrays. Many plans, sketches and maps were drawn to illustrate such proposals. In 1910 the idea was advanced by the St Just and Falmouth Ocean Wharves and Railway Company, but the First World War put an end to that idea. In 1919 it was revised as the St Just Docks Scheme, by which it was envisaged that transatlantic liners would land passengers to travel to London by rail using a newly built line to St Austell. However, by 1923 the *Penryn Advertiser* described this as 'recently abandoned'. Again, in 1939, Silley Cox and Company purchased Messack Farm and promoted a Parliamentary Bill to develop this stretch of shoreline, and after the Second World War the Falmouth Consolidation Bill of 1958–9 referred to the proposed dock complex as 'Messackside'. With the worsening depression in world shipping after the 1960s the entire scheme was forgotten, to leave this magnificent estuary unsullied by unsightly industrial development.

Mylor Creek

Extending about a mile west from what Boazio (see p. 8) described as 'Myler Pool' is Mylor Creek, which, after a narrow entrance, opens into a wide expanse of sheltered water at high tide, but mostly mud at low water. As with most creeks on the estuary, a ferry once ran across its entrance from Roundwood Quay to Mylor Church Town, in order to shorten the traveller's journey at a time when most travel was on foot or on horseback.

The valley east of Mylor church has been owned in turn by the Killigrews and their successors, the Wodehouse family, the Enys family, who bought it, and the Trefusis family, who exchanged it for a parcel of land near the Enys estate. In its natural state the lower end of the valley was a swamp into which flowed a stream from the hills to the south. In the early years of the nineteenth century the Falmouth Packet Establishment was expanding rapidly. When, during the Napoleonic Wars, it became necessary for the Navy to blockade the French Breton ports, Falmouth was the obvious base for such operations. However, the port was so busily engaged with its post office work that the Navy decided to establish its own base near Mylor church. Newspapers of 1805 report the purchase of 13 acres of land from Lord Wodehouse and the building of a cooperage (all water carried on board ships was in barrels), a pier of 90 ft in length, a masthouse, a boathouse, a pitchhouse, a slipway and dwelling houses for the officers. On the hillside above, a reservoir with a pipeline down to the dockyard was laid out in 1806. Soon afterwards a victualling office was set up and regular advertisements appeared in the local newspapers requiring tenders for the supply of fresh vegetables. With the end of the Napoleonic Wars, operations ceased until the Falmouth Packet Establishment, by then controlled by the Navy, began to use the dockyard and several vessels were 'coppered' there, instead of having to go to Plymouth. In the 1841 Census return, seven naval personnel are recorded as residents at the dockyard, and four years later the Navy gave land for a churchyard extension. There was a short-lived reopening for the Crimean War in 1850 and a new house was built for the 'superintendent of Mylor Royal Dockyard'. A gift of land was made for a further churchyard extension in 1871. Many of the original buildings were taken over in 1866 as part of the shore base for HMS *Ganges* (see pp. 14 & 15), and after its departure the Admiralty maintained control. The picture above shows the dockyard and its buildings soon after 1900 with the loaded passenger vessel *Alexandra* steaming out

of Mylor Creek. The wooded valley running inland from the dockyard and Mylor church are on the extreme right. In November 1927 'pier, jetty, waiting rooms, six acres of agricultural and woodland, Admiralty Cottage, the guardhouse, hospital buildings, old Admiralty House plus reservoir holding 168,000 gallons' were leased to Mr A.N. Bath, but later the property was sold to Colonel Henry Trefusis. Since then it has been transformed into the flourishing Mylor Yacht Harbour, which, apart from other uses during the Second World War, has maintained control to this day. Many of the original buildings of the *Ganges* Establishment still exist, albeit altered for their new uses: the old hospital and stores are flats, the hospital kitchen has become the Ganges Restaurant and the mortuary is a mast store. The early post-war yacht harbour (above) has undergone many changes, as the yachting business has expanded over the past forty years. The building on the end of the pier is now the clubhouse of Mylor Sailing Club, and the tidal water north of the pier has become one of the largest yacht moorings in the estuary. To the west of the old dockyard a new T-shaped jetty was constructed in 1951 by the Ministry of War Transport as an emergency pier, but this has been taken over for more peaceable purposes by the yacht harbour.

The earliest church at Mylor is believed to have been at the Cregoes on the top of the hill to the south-east, but of this there remains no trace. Portions of the present Mylor church, shown here, are thought to date back to Norman times. The building is

dedicated to St Melorus, who was reputedly martyred in AD 411. Many alterations to the structure are recorded in the detailed histories of this beautifully sited church, the south porch of which (below) is said to have been taken from Glasney College after its dissolution (see *Lower Fal*, pp. 122–3). The most extensive renovation was carried out in 1870, when the church was almost completely restored. Before this there were dormer-like windows in the roof and an oddly shaped, probably wooden, summit to the tower (see above). The south wall was held up by a large granite support, which, during the 1870 renovation, was found to be the Parish Cross, buried head down and used as a buttress. With the help of sailors from HMS *Ganges*, this was dug up to reveal one of the county's largest known monoliths at over 17 ft. It now stands beside the south door (below) with 7 ft buried in the ground.

The cemetery surrounding the church overlooks Mylor Pool. The postcard (above) has a strange caption, the 'dying' referring to the dozen or so ocean-going steamers anchored here after the First World War, waiting for their last journey to the breaker's yard. As with most graveyards there is much local history to be learned from a study of the headstones; here, there are more than the usual number of notable epitaphs. Most poignant is the ornate monument erected by the parishioners to commemorate the tragedy of the *Queen* transport, wrecked on Trefusis Point in January 1814, with the loss of over two hundred lives. Many of the victims were interred here in a mass grave (see *Falmouth*, p. 128). There are also amusing inscriptions, such as that dated 26 November 1770 to shipwright Joseph Crapp, who was apparently the victim of an accident (right), while another tells the sad fate of Thomas James, a respectable eating-house owner and limekiln operator from Flushing, who was innocently rowing home from St Mawes in December 1814. When approached by Customs men he ignored their challenge, and was mortally wounded when they fired at him: 'Official zeal in luckless hour laid wait and wilful, sent the murderous ball of fate; James to his home which late in health he left, wounded returns – of life is soon bereft.' Later the offenders were tried for wilful murder, for which they served a prison sentence.

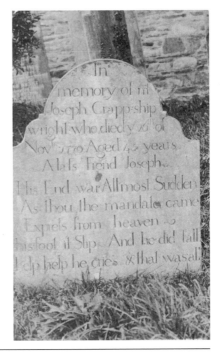

As in many Cornish parishes, a small settlement known as 'Churchtown' grew up around the place of worship. In addition to the vicarage there was usually an inn, in the case of Lawithick the Clinton Arms, which overlooks the church. This was closed when the vicar persuaded the magistrates to refuse it a licence in 1840, as it was attracting a larger attendance than the church. In time it became a tea garden (above), and excursions were run to it from Falmouth by Mr Bell, using the passenger launch *Ibis* (below), which in 1906 was said to be the first passenger vessel on the estuary powered by an internal combustion engine.

To the west of the former dockyard and church, Mylor Creek extends a mile to the village of Mylor Bridge. On the south shore is Trelew Creek. It was here, in 1878, that Thomas Gray, a master shipwright from Porthleven, dug a saw-pit near the road and employed two labourers and two sawyers to build the ketch *Hobah* (above). When the vessel was finished the yard was abandoned. No trace is visible today, but Thomas Gray set up a more permanent yard, called Well Yard, near the top of Falmouth High Street at Well Beach on the north side of Pye's Cellars. For thirty years *Hobah* was owned by Gray and sailed 'deep water' to ports in Western Europe, including trips to Gibraltar with Penryn granite for harbour construction. Repairs were carried out in Well Yard. Basil Greenhill, in his authoritative book *West Country Coasting Ketches*, describes *Hobah* as 'a fine, fast vessel'. In 1908 it was sold for coastal use to owners in Appledore, who fitted it with an engine, but it continued to frequent Cornish waters. As recently as 1937 the ketch discharged coal on the beach at Porthluney, below Caerhayes Castle, and is believed to have been the last vessel to have done this in Cornwall. *Hobah*'s last voyage was in its fifty-second year when, after several breakdowns on a trip from Penarth to Appledore, it was laid up in the Torridge and allowed to rot away.

Mylor grew up around its bridge (above), which was built in 1590. It is referred to on the Boazio map (see p. 6) as 'New bridge', while a document of 1613 refers to the site as 'Ponsnowith' meaning 'new bridge', which is probably the origin of Penoweth, a name still used in the village today. As with all creek-head bridges, it was built at the upper tidal limit on the packhorse and cattle route between Truro and Penryn Market. In 1950 it was widened to satisfy the requirements of modern traffic.

Just below the bridge on the south shore is that part of the village known as Tregatreath, at a point where a tributary stream joins the creek. Believed to have been built by the Lemon family as almshouses in about 1750, the building was later enlarged to become a farm, at which time it faced away from the creek with its entrance looking out on to the Bowling Green. By the mid-twentieth century it was in a state of disrepair, when it was reclaimed by Terry Heard who established a now-flourishing boatyard on the site.

Mill Quay marks the site of a former water-mill fed by a leat that took water from the Mylor stream half a mile above the bridge and ran through the village below the present car park, before working the water-wheel behind the quay. There was also a tide mill nearby on the creek, the dam for which was roughly on the site of the present stepping stones, known to some former villagers as the 'dam stones'. The limekiln on the quay used limestone imported by sailing vessels that also brought in coal for Captain Joe Pearce, whose sheds on the quay housed a wheelbarrow with which customers could take the coal home. Exports included bricks made in the kilns along Comfort Road on the present site of Brick Hill.

Mylor, as with most villages up to the 1920s, was almost entirely self-sufficient. All of the tradesmen lived in the village – blacksmith, carpenter, bricklayer and five cobblers, the latter necessary because most people walked everywhere. The earliest outside transport was a donkey-cart to Flushing, which linked with the ferry to Falmouth. Later a two-horse bus ran until the First World War. During that war many men were introduced to the internal combustion engine, and after 1918 there was a great surplus of vehicles and many men able to drive them. Thus the earliest village buses were converted army vehicles, but in 1927 the Hearle family began running the Riviera service from Mylor to Falmouth with this twenty-seater Thorneycroft (above), seen at its usual stop outside Bert Eskett-Williams's Ash View Supply Stores. This bus ran a regular twenty minute service to Falmouth Moor. This is about as long as the journey takes today but, although there was hardly any other traffic in those days, the poorly surfaced roads were in places only 6 in. wider than the bus. Passengers on the first bus each day were dock workers, and this bus always brought back the bread for Bert Williams's shop from Addison's bakery in Falmouth, also transporting children to the secondary schools, farmers to market, wives going shopping and villagers visiting the cinema. In those days there were two 'houses', and the departure of the last bus depended entirely on the time the cinema programme finished. The service came to an end in 1947 and the fares of 6d. for a single and 9d. for a return had remained unchanged for twenty years.

This building in the heart of the village began its life in 1829 as the Poor House, for which Sir Charles Lemon granted a ninety-nine year lease for a rent of 1d. a year. Soon after it was enlarged in 1834 changes in Poor Law administration meant that it was replaced by the Falmouth Union Workhouse. Sir Charles Lemon, who had previously established a school in New Row, then gave the building as a village school, a gift carried on by his heir, Colonel Tremayne. The clock tower was erected in 1845, and was based on the pattern of a clock tower at Enys (see p. 33). Like most buildings in the village it was built of stone dug from a quarry beside the creek, just east of the village. After the 1902 Education Act the school was taken over by the Board of Education, but a serious fire in 1921 meant that the children had to be educated in the chapels in the village until the present school was constructed in 1924. This brought to an end what must have been something of a record achievement by the Ashton family, three generations of which had occupied the post of headmaster for eighty years, between 1845 and 1925.

After Mylor School was destroyed by fire it was rebuilt as the Tremayne Hall, for use by the village. This picture shows the British Legion's Children's Party in the new hall, decorated to celebrate its opening on 23 April 1925.

Just out of the village on the Penryn road is this impressive house, Woodlands, which was built in about 1803 by Rear Admiral Bartholomew James after his retirement from active service in 1801. After his death in 1828 another famous naval family, the Sulivans, is believed to have lived here, several members of which are buried in Mylor churchyard. By 1893 the house had become the home of Harry Pike, a market gardener, who seasonally employed several village ladies to pick and bunch daffodils, anemones and violets, and to pick tomatoes grown under glass. Most of the produce was taken to Penryn station by horse-wagon, bound for Covent Garden, although some was sent by bus to Boase, the fruiterer and florist, at Market Strand, Falmouth. Harry Pike had a sailing barge called *Skipper* in which he used to transport manure from the stables of the Greenbank Hotel in Falmouth. During this latter period the house was said to have been haunted by a young girl, who would run from the house and throw herself into the lake.

Although much of the village of Mylor Bridge was part of the Carclew estate for many years, the nearest stately home to the village is Enys, home of the family of the same name that has lived in the district since the thirteenth century. In addition to owning much property in the nearby port of Penryn, the estate at one time had land on the Lizard, in Roseland and north of Truro, but the family suffered from its Royalist support during the Civil War. The family name was perpetuated in 1802 only when the widow, Lucy Anne Hunt, was authorized to re-assume her maiden name. After the old Tudor house (above) was burned down in 1826, the present house (below) was built, in 1830. Reservoirs were constructed in the gardens, with water-wheels, made by Rapsons of Penryn, to pump water to the house. On those occasions when the gardens are opened in aid of charity, these can still be seen.

The lodge house (above), shown in 1905, stands on the Penryn road and is still occupied today. The library (below) shows that Enys House was the home of a highly cultured family. Much of the collection of books, maps, documents and pamphlets, known as the Enys Collection, was presented to Falmouth Library early in the twentieth century, then transferred to the County Records Office in the 1960s.

In the late 1930s plans to make the estate more remunerative included letting the house. After 1940, when the Netherlands had been occupied by the Germans, the Dutch Naval Authorities took over Enys as their Royal Naval College, until it could be re-established in their own country after the Second World War, in 1946. These pictures show the Dutch Naval Cadets studying in the library (above) and on parade, outside the main door (right). To commemorate their fond association with this house, the present Royal Dutch Naval Institute at Den Helder has recently named a new building Enys House.

In 1749 Mr William Lemon, the rich Truro mine-owner and merchant, purchased the Carclew estate, which included the village of Mylor Bridge, and the unfinished Carclew House from James Bonython. The completed house (above) is represented in an engraving by William Borlase, presented by Mr Lemon for the *Natural History of Cornwall* in 1758. In 1760 his grandson, later Sir William Lemon, inherited the estate and was succeeded by his second son, Sir Charles Lemon (below), in 1824. In 1868 a nephew of Sir Charles, Colonel Arthur Tremayne, a survivor of the Charge of the Light Brigade, inherited. He was succeeded by his son, Captain William Tremayne, in 1905.

On the north side, the Carclew estate ran down to Restronguet Creek and in the early decades of the nineteenth century the development of the port of Devoran and the expansion of mining in the creek led Sir William Lemon to observe: 'Unwilling as I am to have the river again defaced and all my comforts at Carclew broken in upon by tinners going all over my grounds . . . I must not bear the odium of discouraging mining in Cornwall.'

The magnificent Carclew House (above) was built near the top of the hill between Mylor and Restronguet creeks, surrounded by trees and open parkland. The first owner, often known as the 'great' William Lemon, came from a Germoe family and entered mining as the manager of the smelting house at Chyandour, Penzance. His investments in the appropriately named Wheal Fortune, together with a substantial dowry from his marriage to Isabella Vibert, enabled him to move to Truro, where, in 1739, he built what was soon regarded as the finest town house in Truro, Prince's House, between the Coinage Hall and the quays. The garden ran down to the River Kenwyn (near the site of the present Pannier Market), at a time when the tide ran up to Lemon Street (see p. 141). Shrewd investments in the Gwennap copper mines (including the building of the County Adit) enabled him to branch out into commerce and banking. Ten years later he bought and completed the construction of Carclew House, which had lain unfinished for twenty years. This marked William Lemon's entry into the landed gentry and, aided by his wife, he laid out the estate as parkland. They lived here in the summer season when town living was very unhealthy, but moved to Truro for the winter when the condition of the roads made travel difficult and uncomfortable. The elegant house, inherited by his grandson, later Sir William Lemon, became the venue for a hectic social life, with its large, columned entrance hall, broad staircase and seven bedrooms. In 1923 *Kelly's Directory* said of Carclew, when it was the seat of Captain William Tremayne DL, JP: 'the exterior has a noble appearance, the south front opening to a sweep of lawn lined with masses of drooping foliage: the west front overlooks a wooded valley, bounded by distant hills. The deer park and plantations occupy an area of over a square mile and the approach to the house is through an avenue of lofty trees a mile long'. Unfortunately, tragedy was soon to strike.

At 2.00 a.m. on 5 April 1934, fire mysteriously broke out and spread quickly, so that Captain Tremayne's family, guests and servants barely escaped in their nightclothes and could only stand on the lawn, watching the blaze. The telephone lines had been destroyed by the fire and the chauffeur had to drive to Falmouth to alert the fire brigade, who, together with the Truro firemen, toiled bravely but were unable to save the house from total destruction. Today (left) the ivy-covered remains of the west wing stand on the hilltop. The estate lands were sold off, some for farming and some for housing development.

Restronguet Creek

Weir Beach marks the entrance to the most extensive and, at one time, most intensely industrialized creek on the estuary. Navigable tidal water once reached 4 miles inland, as far as Bissoe Bridge and Perran Wharf, but mining activity has caused extensive silting and any access today is restricted to only the very highest of spring tides. The beach is covered at high tide when the right of way passes behind the wall, where the masts of the yachts are a reminder that Restronguet Sailing Club had its headquarters here before moving farther south to near Mylor dockyard in 1962. The old house pictured here has been demolished and replaced by modern development.

The narrow entrance to Restronguet Creek is seen here from the hill above Weir Beach. Five Falmouth Working Boats, probably used for oyster dredging, lie at anchor in the foreground, while on the far side of the entrance the road from Harcourt and Porthgwidden winds down to the end of Restronguet Point, as it does today. From this road a ferry ran to two destinations on the south shore (see p. 42): one to Weir Beach (the mast of which can be seen at the bottom of the picture); the other to the inn (see p. 41, at the bottom of the steep hill leading to Mylor Bridge and Penryn). From this entrance, barely 220 yards wide, the creek widens to a magnificent body of water known as Restronguet Pool (see p. 41, above). This was described in 1827 by R. Thomas in his *History of Falmouth* as 'an excellent and well sheltered anchorage with four to six fathoms of water at low tide: here many Norwegian vessels discharge cargoes of timber'. Destined for mines in the creek's hinterland, this timber would have been rafted up on the high tide to Devoran or Perran Wharf, near the present Norway Inn. On the far shore a projection below the farthest house marks the site of Marblehead Quay, still well preserved today. This, as with many other such quays on the estuary, was used for loading copper and tin ore for export and unloading imported timber and coal.

Restronguet Pool is seen at its widest from between the two ferry termini at Weir and Restronguet Passage. Projecting from the south shore (far left) is Strangweke Quay, which is believed to have been the origin of the name 'Restronguet' (see p. 42). On the far shore, above the mast of the anchored Working Boat, once stood the famous boatyard at the appropriately named Yard Point. This was operated by the master craftsman William 'Foreman' Ferris, who was responsible for building so many of the fine sailing vessels that traded in and out of the estuary.

The Pandora Inn, today a well-known and popular hostelry, was first a farm and later the Passage House Inn. It was renamed 'Pandora' by Captain Edwards, an ex-Naval officer who was sent to bring the *Bounty* mutineers back to this country. His vessel, *Pandora*, was wrecked on the Barrier Reef, as a result of which he was dismissed from the service and came to Cornwall. He bought the inn and renamed it after his lost ship.

The view above, from the north side of the creek, shows a bell in the foreground from the Chellew Line vessel SS *Penpol*, which was rung to summon the ferry from the other side. To the right of the terrace of houses on the far shore is Strangweke Quay, leased by the Fox foundry at Perran in 1789 and used as a transhipment point for coal and timber imports bound for Perran Wharf. Heavy lifting gear was installed for loading on to ocean-going ships the machinery brought down by lighters and boilers, made watertight and floated down the creek. From this quay in 1880 the last Cornish engine to be manufactured at Perran foundry was shipped. The 70 in. cylinder was loaded on the schooner *Voltung* for passage to Barrow-in-Furness. Perran foundry was closed that same year. The picture below shows a regatta taking place at high tide off the Pandora Inn, with several Working Boats and a passenger tug in attendance. Next to the inn is the hill responsible for the fact that beer had at one time to be delivered by boat, as the slope was too steep for dray horses to negotiate.

This view, probably from the beach at Yard Point on the eastern shore of the entrance to Penpol Creek, shows the degree of industrialization in the village of Point. The tall chimney on the left was part of the disused lead smelter, the red bricks of which were used after the chimney had been demolished in about 1910 to build the pair of houses still to be seen behind Daniell's Quay. To the right is the stack of the still-operating tin smelting works, which, although by far the smallest of the four Cornish smelters still operating, carried on production until 1921. The chimney was demolished in the early 1930s.

After the Second World War, as part of the disposal of surplus and obsolete naval craft, these were three of a total of nine submarines dumped on a very high tide on the mud in various parts of Restronguet Creek. They were (right to left) HMS *Terrapin*, HMS *Thresher* and HMS *Tribune*. Another, HMS *Tuna*, had become famous for its part in the landing of Royal Marine commandos in the River Gironde in south-western France to blow up German shipping in Bordeaux, an operation commemorated in the film *Cockleshell Heroes*. Eventually, after protests from creekside residents, the vessels were removed.

This copy of a watercolour hanging in the Royal Institution of Cornwall in Truro, and reproduced by their permission, shows the extent to which the now peaceful shore of Penpol Creek was at one time covered with industrial buildings. Space precludes a fully detailed description (available in Viv Acton's book *Years of Change in Point and Penpol*), but this 1857 view shows, on the left, the lead smelting works in production at Point, with its high chimney looming over Lemon Quay and its sheds. Smaller chimneys to the right along the creekside are likely to be the ancillary works, such as the smithy and desilvering works. The lead ore was brought in on the horsedrawn 'tram' from Devoran (see pp. 46 & 47), although some was imported from other parts of the country and overseas. As some of the Cornish ore was geologically described as 'argentiferous', silver was an important by-product of the smelting process, and a newspaper report of 1863 casually mentions the existence of 'a lump of silver weighing half a ton'. Increasing competition from overseas sources caused lead prices to fall, and by 1871 production here had almost ceased. The works was put up for sale in 1873, by which time tin smelting had begun in the creekside buildings to the right. Tin ore was brought from the Redruth area by steam train to Devoran and on to the Penpol works via the 'tram', and some was crushed in stamps and concentrated using the old Cornish 'buddle' on the quayside. A tall chimney to remove arsenical fumes was built on the hillside on the extreme right ('Stack Lane' is still there today), connected to the furnaces by underground flues, traces of which may still be found in the gardens of houses occupying the site. Competition from cheaper overseas tin spelled the end of the industry in Cornwall but the picture shows clearly what a busy and prosperous industrial area this quiet creek was 150 years ago.

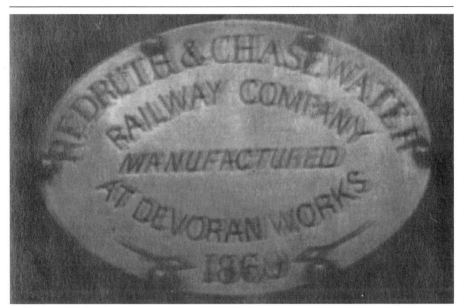

Entirely responsible for the growth of Devoran was the Redruth and Chasewater Railway, so named in the Parliamentary Bill that promoted it in 1823 (although the planned spur line to Chacewater never materialized). It was opened along its entire length for use between Redruth and Devoran in 1826. Parts of it had been used before this date. Up until 1854 it was operated by horses, but after that date steam engines were used, although the sidings down to the wharfside at Devoran and the 'tram' to Point continued to use horses. The brass plate (above) was attached to the locomotive *Miner* after it had been completely rebuilt in the company's new Devoran repair sheds in 1869. The view below shows the route followed by the straight railway line through the inland part of the quays as far east as Narabo Quay and Tallack's Creek. This has become a road bordered by houses, but traces of the granite sleepers used to support the rails are still visible in places.

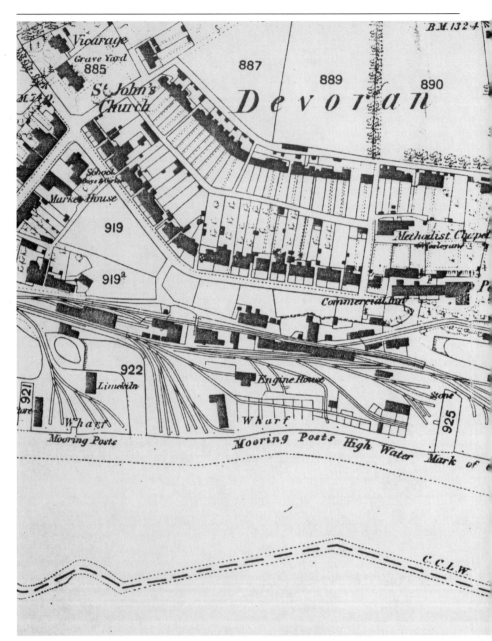

Looking at Devoran today it is difficult to imagine that two hundred years ago nothing but open fields bordered the muddy creek, while eighty years later Cornwall's busiest port had grown up. This extract from the OS map of 1880 (25 miles to 1 inch) shows the extent of both industrial and residential development, much of it illustrated in the following pages. Points of particular interest here are: the wharves and mooring posts along the whole creekside; the excavated inlets dug into the shore to increase wharf

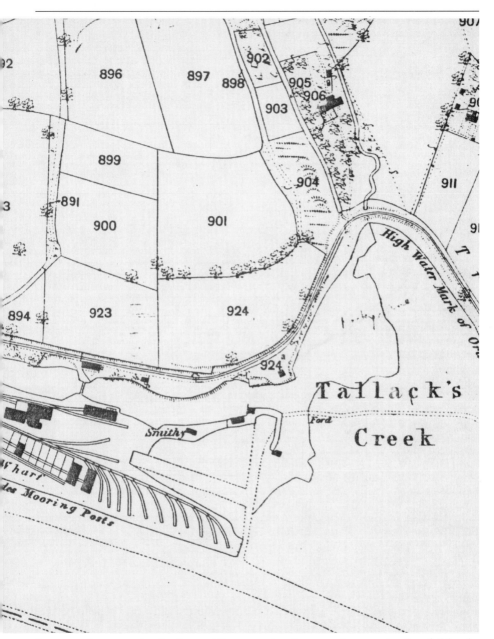

frontage; the network of railway sidings running down to the water's edge, fed by the Redruth and Chasewater Railway and the buildings associated with the railway; the horse-operated 'tram' running east around Tallack's Creek towards Point; buildings such as the 'smithy', 'coal store' and 'lime kiln'; and the residential development along two parallel terraces on the hillside above the waterfront, planned by the Agar-Robartes of Lanhydrock, the landowners.

This picture of high tide at Devoran, probably dating from the early twentieth century, shows clearly several of the features seen on the west end of the map (see pp. 46 & 47). On the higher ground there are the residential terraces with their access to the waterside, and Market Street (formerly Lemon Street), running downhill on the left. As in most settlements up to the late nineteenth century, sanitation was rudimentary. In 1893 this, combined with a somewhat defective water supply, led to an outbreak of cholera, which moved the Revd Tom Philpotts (see p. 81) to write to the agent of the landowners about the problem of sewage disposal and drainage, and speedy action was taken. The spire on the skyline locates the church, built in 1855–6, and the tall building to its right is the school, built in 1846 and used for divine services until the church was built. Below the school is the market house, in which, according to *Kelly's Directory* of 1893, 'a market for meat and vegetables is held on Fridays, a small stone building erected by Lord Robartes, but it is very sparsely attended. The Library and Reading Rooms, over the Market Hall, are supplied with the local papers and magazines and there is a small attached library.' Devoran was part of Feock Parish until 1873, when it became an ecclesiastical parish in its own right. Along the waterfront are the various industrial and commercial buildings, most noticeable of which is the long dark engine repair shed, now converted into the attractively functional village hall. The sailing vessel on the right, only able to reach this far upstream at high tide, lies off the entrance to an inlet similar to that numbered 922 on the map. On the extreme right the building with the arched entrance is probably the limekiln named on the map, one of many round the estuary built to supply lime for building purposes and for farmers in the hinterland, who used it to reduce the acidity of the soil.

This low-tide view of Devoran waterfront extends farther downstream to the east to show, on the extreme right, the ore bins of 'hutches' on Narabo Quay, the last to survive. Originally the railway sidings ran on wooden supports over these stone-built box-like structures, into which ore was fed from trucks known as 'deeps', the bottom of which opened to allow the ore to fall through. The wooden piles along the wharfside, used instead of stone facing as pile driving was easy in the soft mud, show signs of neglect and collapse. Although there are two topsail schooners resting on the mud, this picture probably dates from when the port was in decline after 1870. Having reached its commercial peak in the 1840s, when it was the busiest port in the county, exporting copper ore and importing coal and timber, there began a slow decline as cheaper foreign ore posed an increasing threat to the deeper Cornish mines, which were becoming more and more expensive to drain. In April 1877 the *West Briton* reported: 'The trade at this little port is in a miserable plight just now. It has fallen off and where ten vessels used to enter and discharge, scarcely one does now. This arises from the failure of the Consols, United, Clifford and other mines which at one time formed some of the largest concerns in the county employing directly and indirectly thousands of hands and they were supplied mainly from the port of Devoran. It may almost be said that the whole district is shut up from a mining point of view and the consequence is that there is no copper ore to ship . . . and no coal brought back. . . . Better times are anxiously longed for.' Some aspects of the port's activities were, however, managing to survive. In March 1875 it was reported that shipbuilding was growing and the first schooner built there by Mr Hugh Stephens, of 240 tons, was the largest built inside Restronguet Creek for a Welsh company: 'a large concourse of people assembled to see her off the stocks'. Based on Devoran, there was also 'an extensive trade done in the cultivation of oysters by Messrs T. Kemp and Company, who supply the London and other markets from their beds in the River Fal'. Although much of the old Devoran port has been engulfed by the tide of 'development' in the past four decades, the extreme eastern end of the dock has been saved from this fate by the strenuous efforts of the Devoran Quay Preservation Society, whose members during a period of two years (1987–9), raised a large sum to buy the quay and then protect it against erosion by the sea. All credit is due to them for having saved this valuable piece of local history, which is now open for all to enjoy.

For nearly thirty years after 1826 the Redruth and Chasewater line used horse traction, but in 1854, after some adjustments to the line, two identical 0–4–0 saddle-tank locomotives were unloaded from Glasgow. They were appropriately named *Miner* (above) and *Smelter*, and became operative on 1 December of that year. After a year's operations the track below Nangiles had to be overhauled as a result of the extra weight of the engines, and parts of the line were replaced on account of excessive wear. In 1857 the mileage was over 23,000 miles, almost equally shared between the two locomotives, but the hot cinders thrown out on the steeper gradients involved the company in replacing all of the thatched houses along the route with tiled roofs. *Miner* was rebuilt in 1869 with a rear removable weatherboard (above), but it was not popular with the drivers and was therefore removed (below). The plaque (see p. 45) is clearly visible in both pictures.

Smelter (above) is outside the Devoran Loco shed (see p. 52) with one of its doors open in the background. The boiler is covered with repair patches. This locomotive did not share the 1869 transformation with *Miner* and was eventually relegated to emergency work only. In 1859 a third, heavier, locomotive was bought from Glasgow. Named *Spitfire* (below), it was used at first on the steeper part of the line above Nangiles. After having new brass tubes fitted it ran over 11,000 miles in 1864, as far as the other two locomotives combined. A major overhaul in the early 1890s was something of a disaster and the engine's efficiency was considerably reduced. In 1918 all three were sold for scrap after *Miner* had performed the sorry task of lifting the track, which was also scrapped.

Among the many buildings that formed part of the railway operation, two of the 1920s are shown here. Above is the engine shed in which the locomotives were kept overnight. The original wooden building was destroyed by fire in 1863 and this stone structure replaced it. The building was in use as a coal store in the 1920s but has now been demolished and a bungalow built on the site. Many of the road crossings on the line had an adjoining house in which the keeper lived. Below, the crossing over the Truro Turnpike at the north end of the embankment over the Carnon Valley, built in 1827, is shown. The house has only recently been demolished in road-widening operations, but the gate, albeit in a very sorry condition, is still to be seen beside the busy A39 road.

Workers on the railway included train crews, ballast men, plate-layers, switch men, crossing keepers, as well as these six men and three boys (above), who worked in the wagon and locomotive repair sheds. Down near Tallack's Creek was a smithy, where the horses used on the tram were shod. One of these horses, its handler and the blacksmith (right) are shown below. The stables were on Narabo Quay. Horses were also used in shunting wagons on the network of sidings on the quays.

Navigation for large vessels such as the topsail schooners shown here was always somewhat hazardous in the upper reaches of the creek, even at high tide. Cargoes were brought up to Devoran Quays whenever possible, but larger vessels would lie in Restronguet Pool near the creek mouth and either tranship the cargo into lighters, such as that shown here, lying off the bow of the schooner, or, with timber, throw it over the side to be rafted up to Devoran, where it was seasoned in the timber pools or sent up to the mines.

To overcome the problem of a lack of wind, which often had vessels waiting up to ten days in Restronguet Pool, the railway company purchased a wooden-hulled tug, *Sydney*, in 1847, which was soon sunk in a collision and needed extensive repairs. A larger tug, *Pendennis*, shown here, was added to the fleet in 1858. Both tugs were managed by the Port of Falmouth Steam Tug Company and were used for passengers as well as towage until *Sydney* was sold overseas in 1870 and *Pendennis* to East Anglian owners in 1877, as the registration shows. This picture is reproduced by permission of Alan Kittridge.

Many smaller sailing vessels were used in the creek for a variety of purposes. The barge *Mary* is shown (left) in full sail, approaching the wharves at high tide while the vessel (right) is high and dry at low tide in one of the inlets along the Devoran waterfront, with sails furled and nine men, crew and porters. The picture below is particularly interesting as it shows both embankments of the original Carnon stream works against a background of Carclew Woods. The 25 ton *Mary* was built in 1875 in the Devoran yard, beside Tallack's Creek. Such vessels were known locally as barges and used to carry general cargo like roadstone, sand, corn, bricks, coal and fertilizer. Operated by two very hard-worked crew, they plied to the head of every creek in the estuary.

These pictures epitomize nagivation in Restronguet Creek in the latter days of Devoran Docks. Above, the steamer *Beta* is tied up to a wharfside granite bollard, some of which are still *in situ* along the much-changed creek shore. Astern of this vessel lies a topsail schooner. On the wharf is one of the railway wagons known as 'deeps', while off the bow of the steamer is a small section of one of the embankments of the Carnon stream works. Below, *Erimus*, a Falmouth-registered steamer, leaves the wharves to proceed down the creek. With the decline of the mines for which the railway had originally been built, both *Erimus* and *Trefusis* were used in the 1890s to carry coal from Swansea for the few surviving mines and for domestic use in Redruth. The last time a vessel used the quay at Devoran was in 1916, when a small schooner unloaded coal for Redruth gasworks. After 1918 the quays slowly collapsed as their wooden piles rotted away, wharves became overgrown and channels silted up.

Viewed here from the south shore of the creek, three steamers lie aground on the mud at low tide off Narabo Quay at the eastern end of Devoran Docks, demonstrating one of the main problems experienced at the port. Navigation in the creek became increasingly difficult as sediment poured down the Carnon River from the mines upstream and from the County Adit. The railway company carried out some dredging operations, especially of the upper wharves, and its tug *Pendennis* (see p. 54) was equipped with mud-rakes after 1858 which, towed behind the vessel on an ebb tide, removed some of the sediment. Eventually a sluice-pond was installed at the extreme western end, beside the turnpike road, in which water was ponded at high tide to be released at each low tide to surge down the navigable channel and carry mud with it. The remains of this pond and its sluice-gate, albeit silted up, can still be seen beside the A39 road. Another source of silt in the creek itself was the presence, at different times, of three mines extracting alluvial tin from a rich deposit under the mud. Between 1822 and 1874 these mines exploited this deposit at different points along the creek: Upper Carnon mine (1822–7), with the remains of its engine house still standing on the eastern shore of Tallack's Creek; Lower Carnon mine (1833–43) off Yard Point, which incorporated a man-made island in midstream through which a shaft was sunk and which can be seen today at low tide as the 'mine bank'; and the Restronguet Creek Tin Stream Company (1871–4), off Point Quay, which also had a midstream island, the only remains of which today are the projecting stumps of timber that once supported the 'iron shaft'.

From Devoran the Redruth and Chasewater Railway ran 8½ miles, up the Carnon Valley to Nangiles where it crossed the valley on an embankment and climbed gradually up towards Crofthandy and Carharrack. Here it crossed the road at the top of Lanner Hill before dropping down into Redruth. *Miner* is seen in this picture hauling eighteen wagons along the level valley floor below Twelveheads. Above this point the gradient steepens up towards Goongumpus, as a result of which the wagons were taken up in two batches of nine. The plate (see p. 45) was fixed on the side of the locomotive cab after the engine was rebuilt in the company's new repair shop in 1869. It was converted to an 0–6–0 arrangement and had the frame lengthened to give the weight required for more efficient operation on the steeper part of the line. Much of the route of this famous old mineral line can still be walked, and in places the old granite sleepers remain in their original position. The copper boom between 1800 and 1860 proved the inadequacy of the mule trains previously employed to carry the ore to the many quays on the Fal Estuary for shipment to the South Wales foundries, so this 4 ft gauge line was opened in 1826. After 1866 foreign competition resulted in a gradual decline in copper production at mines such as Clifford Amalgamated, with its eighteen steam engines, which closed in 1870. Reduced trade on the railway and at Devoran Docks resulted, but down-traffic continued, albeit on a smaller scale, with ingot tin for export to Liverpool, black tin for the Penpol smelter, bricks from St Day, and chemicals and arsenic from the Bissoe chemical works. Up-traffic was mainly coal for the Bassett mines.

One of three serious accidents that occurred on the line was in March 1899 near the Carnon Bridge road crossing. Empty coal wagons left on the track near the Bissoe vitriol works were being pushed ahead of a train going down towards Devoran, when newly laid chippings at the road crossing caused their derailment. The resulting pile-up caused the brakeman, Stephen Gay, to receive fatal injuries. The gatekeeper on duty at the time was his sister-in-law, and the engine driver was his father-in-law. Two other fatal accidents took place. In 1876, near the old Steam Engine Inn at Carharrack, an old lady was struck on the road crossing. At the same place, seventeen years later, a train hit a fully laden greengrocer's cart.

At most of the road crossings on the line a gate was manned, usually by a lady living in the adjacent house. The keeper's duties were clearly laid down in the company's rules and regulations, which specified that she had to be in attendance at 7.00 a.m., or as much earlier as may be required, and had to remain until the passing of the last train. Locomotives indicated their approach by blasts on the whistle, at which the keeper would close the road until the train had passed. *Spitfire* (above) is crossing the road at Bissoe Bridge, with an interested group of bystanders. Below is the Helston road crossing on Buller Downs, with the lady keeper on what is believed to be one of the last trains to run on the Redruth and Chasewater Railway, in 1915.

With the sale of the Perran foundry by the Fox family in 1851, the new owners reduced the staff and some workers banded together to establish the Bassett foundry, a mile downstream near the junction of the Carnon and Perran Valleys, just south of the formerly tidal Tarrandean Creek. The business was never very successful during this period of depression in Cornish mining and closed in 1876, even though the owners had improved the water supply to the foundry with an extended leat that led to the water-wheel driving their forge. A short-lived occupation by the Cornwall and Devon Chemical Manure and Bone Works ended in 1882, but an advertisement for its sale included, significantly, 'having the advantage of a river frontage for barges'. In 1895, after three years of disuse, the site was acquired by Walter Visick, a member of a local family and a worker at Williams's Perran foundry until its closure in 1879. Problems with water power were solved in 1905 with the erection of the undershot water-wheel (above), combined with the installation of a dam on the Mellingey stream (also above), which enclosed a reservoir of about 11 acres to the north of the building shown in the picture. The Visick family survived the mining depression, which, with the silting of the port of Devoran, was destroying all other industrial and commercial activity in the area. They succeeded by specializing in products for both public works and domestic use. The former comprised manhole covers, lampposts, gratings and drain covers, while the latter included cooking ranges, railings, and weights for sash windows. Three generations of the family kept the business going through two world wars, during which considerable contributions were made to the 'war effort'. Between 1915 and 1918 much ship repair work was subcontracted to the firm from Falmouth Docks, while the Second World War saw the production of components for Bailey Bridges and castings for gun mountings. Post-war developments saw diversification into pressed steel components for house building, but the construction of the Ross Bridge in Penzance and the harbour gate at Charlestown were the company's most prestigious contracts. The engineering slump of the 1980s saw the demise of the company and, despite a short-lived takeover by the King Harry Steam Ferry Company in 1987, engineering soon ceased on the site after nearly a century of production at the Bassett Works.

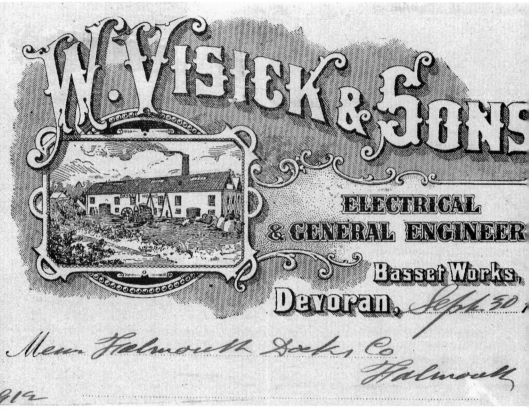

W. VISICK & SONS

ELECTRICAL
& GENERAL ENGINEER

Basset Works,
Devoran, Sept 30

Mess Falmouth Docks Co
Falmouth

Today, a journey along the Carnon Valley between Devoran and Twelveheads gives no idea of the changes that have taken place in this 3 mile stretch of valley floor. Tidal water reached Bissoe Bridge up to about the year 1600, but sedimentation from the mines in the hills above, alluvial mining in the tidal creek itself and the 1768 opening of the County (Great) Adit, eventually with its 30 miles of interconnecting tunnels draining more than thirty-five mines, had filled the valley floor by the early 1800s. After that date a proliferation of industrial activity, some encouraged by the building of the Redruth and Chasewater Railway, included the Bassett Engineering Works, the decorative letter head of which is shown above, and the Carnon Chemical Works, described in *Kelly's Directory* of 1893 as 'manufacturers of the best refined white powdered arsenic, ochre for paper and paint-makers, oxide of iron for the purification of gas and tungstate of soda'. Lead and tin smelting took place near Bissoe Bridge and the square stack of the Bissoe Arsenic Company is still standing. At several points along the valley floor copper precipitation works were established to extract the abundant copper from solution in the river water. The process used was that first employed by Richard Symons in 1854, in which the water was made to flow over scrap iron, on to which copper was then deposited. Up to 100 tons of pure copper were obtained in some years, and the process was continued into the 1950s.

GENERAL VIEW OF WORKS, FACING WEST, CARNON, FALMOUTH CONSOLIDATED LTD. 70

In addition to the alluvial tin deposits of the Carnon valley floor, lode tin has been extensively mined for centuries on the slopes around the valley. This view of Falmouth Consolidated Ltd, just below Bissoe Bridge (with an error in its caption as the view faces east), shows the valley as it was in about 1910. To the left of the buildings, which old OS maps suggest were vitriol works producing sulphuric acid, the Redruth and Chasewater Railway curves round from Bissoe and straightens out to run south-east under the GWR viaduct. The valley floor has undergone drastic transformation since then as different companies have extracted tin from the sediment. In the distance the Brunel 'fan' Viaduct, with its characteristic wooden superstructure, on the Truro to Falmouth line crosses the valley. Falmouth Consolidated Ltd came into existence in 1905 during the early twentieth-century revival, when much outside capital was invested in Cornish mines because of the high price of tin. There was a belief that the new pumping engines using electricity would be cheaper than coal-burning pumps, but this was proved to be a fallacy. This company, the shares of which were marketed as 'Falcons', took over a combination of the workings of several former mines – Wheal Jane, West Jane, Nangiles, Wheal Widden, Wheal Falmouth and Sperries – some of which had begun their lives as copper mines as early as 1740, but which later produced tin in quantity, with arsenic plentiful in places. The company was dissolved in 1915, but tributers continued working parts of the lodes until 1919.

These views of the Carnon Viaduct, one of the eight originally built on the railway line between Truro and Falmouth, show its wooden superstructure on masonry piers. Problems with its construction entailed sinking very deep foundations as a result of the thickness of sediment in what had been a tidal creek: the central piers were sunk 50 ft deep to reach bedrock. In 1930–3 the instability of the wooden 'fan' structure led to its replacement by a new viaduct with masonry arches alongside the old structure, the pillars of which are still in place. The view above is of particular interest as it shows not only a long GWR passenger train crossing but also the track of the 4 ft gauge Redruth and Chasewater Railway, which pre-dated the line above it by thirty-nine years, at the beginning of its straight run down the valley to Devoran. The lower picture looks west up the valley and shows the extent to which the flat floor was often flooded.

These 1965 pictures show one of the most recent enterprises to extract tin from the sediment on the floor of the Carnon Valley. The old Nangiles engine-house (above) is on the distant skyline. The Bissoe installation of Hydraulic Tin Ltd was one of the last of the firms to work over the tailings in the valley floor, each one using more efficient techniques than the one before and recovering tin their predecessors had left behind. The operations shown in these pictures are the diversion of the Carnon River to prevent contamination with silt during the extraction process (above) and the extraction of sediment to a depth of 20 ft using dragline excavators (below).

Of the many examples of silting in the Fal Estuary, that seen most often is the Perran Creek with the A39 Falmouth to Truro road running alongside it. This low-tide picture shows that it was, in the past, used for navigation when sailing barges brought cargoes from ocean-going vessels in the Lower Fal or Restronguet Pool as far up the creek as possible before transhipment into lighters, such as that shown here alongside the barge. The end of the quay (left) is one of three built beside the turnpike road along the north shore of the creek and having direct access from it. This is probably Sampson's Quay, which was built in 1830 by the builder of Tullimaar House, Benjamin Sampson. Sampson had worked his way up from being a carpenter at Tresavean mine and clerk at Perran foundry to a position of great responsibility as a shareholder in the foundry, in the management of which he was active between 1820 and 1840. More recently the house has been associated with General Dwight Eisenhower during the preparations for the D-Day invasion of France in 1944. Near the sharp bend farther upstream is the pleasant picnic spot of Double Quays, which was a Fox installation used by traffic up to the foundry and, later, by the Edwards family up to the First World War, after which road transport drastically reduced river traffic. Farther downstream, behind what is now the garage on the Devoran embankment road, was Tregaskis's Quay, once a substantial stone jetty with considerable trade but now entirely obscured by silting near the creek junction.

This fascinating engraving shows how very different the area at the head of Perran Creek was in 1830 compared with its appearance today. On the left is the wide tidal creek leading to Carclew Bridge (see p. 74), on the far side of which are the smoking chimneys of Perran foundry. The open water to the right of the bridge was at one time a timber pool in which timber was floated for seasoning, and the enclosed water channel beside the road on the right – still visible today – was the canal leading from lower down the creek to Perran Wharf, located where the building is shown to the right of the sailing boat. The wharf was the earliest commercial enterprise in the creek and was used for the import of the requirements of the local, largely agricultural community, such as coal, guano and timber. Imports of limestone were taken directly to a kiln beside the Norway Inn. A pen-picture of the wharf in the 1820s was painted by Mrs Ellen Crewsdon (née Fox) in her nostalgic account *Our Childhood at Perran*, in which she wrote: 'troops of mules, led by a considerate horse, brought ore from the mines . . . copper ore to inspect as it lay on the wharf . . . rafts of timber . . . pushed by stalwart men . . . echoes of the whole valley with dull loud regular thumps . . . the hammer of the Foundry, worked not by steam . . . little used then, but by the water of the stream which came down from Pons-a-neuth' and 'casts made there of great mine "bobs", requiring twenty-four horses to take them, one at a time, up the hill'. The road on the right was newly built, having been laid by the Turnpike Trust in 1828–9 along the creekside from Goonvrea to the new embankment across the Carnon Valley and up the hill to Carnon Downs. The buildings on the far side of the Norway Inn would have been occupied by workers at the wharf or the foundry. The buildings in the trees (high up on the left) represent the row of houses that is still occupied, known as Foundry Row, but the tower-like structure remains something of a mystery.

This early twentieth-century picture of a horse-bus outside the Norway Inn is very different from the scene at this popular roadside hostelry today. Mentioned in 1829 in both the *Poor Rate Book* and the *Royal Cornwall Gazette*, when the landlord's daughter was burned to death, the inn was marked on the 1841 Tithe Apportionment Map, showing the building with offices – the usual name for what we now call 'conveniences' – outhouses and canal cellars. Trade must have picked up after the turnpike road was completed and it became a staging-post on the new Falmouth to Truro road. The name is believed to derive from its association with the timber ships and their crews bringing cargoes from Norway to Perran Wharf, for use in the mines. There was a quarry – still visible – at the rear of the inn, stone from which was used for house, wall, bridge and road building locally. Adjoining the quarry was a limekiln, raw material for which was brought by lighter to a circular turning basin on the east side of the inn, connected to the canal (see p. 67) by a short junction channel, which the turnpike road had to cross by means of a narrow humpback bridge, familiar to all motorists on the Truro road today. By 1899 the kiln was out of use. The *West Briton* of 20 February 1899 reported that a very high spring tide had flooded the inn. This experience was repeated as recently as 1974.

The roadside hamlet of Perranarworthal at the head of the creek now experiences dense road traffic moving between Falmouth and Truro, but these pictures show it in more tranquil days. Although large houses such as Goonvrea and Tredrea were built on the higher ground overlooking the creek, the houses of the artisans stood nearer their place of work. This row of cottages is known as Riverside, and although they were built for use as homes and offices for the foundry workers they all look much the same today. The tradesman's cart drawn up on the left (right) is evocative of a time earlier this century that has been vividly described in a booklet, written in 1988 by Miss Ivy Edwards at the age of ninety, entitled *The Family at Rose Villa*.

The Fox family established its business in Falmouth in 1769 under the Quaker patriarch George Croker Fox. The astute business sense of this eminent man and his two sons, George Croker and Robert Were, led to the development of Perran Wharf at the head of navigation of Perran Creek. Above Carclew Bridge, perhaps on the site of the former Perran Tin Smelting Works, they later established Perran foundry in 1791, taking advantage of the proximity of the site to the developing copper mines in Gwennap parish. Power was supplied, initially, by the Kennal River, which flows from the Carnmenellis moorland (the site of the present Stithians Reservoir and Dam), through Kennal Vale and Ponsanooth, from which leats were constructed to supply power to water-wheels on both sides of the valley (above). These pictures show the foundry after it had been taken over by the Edwards family in 1890, but many of the features date from foundry days. The 12 ft diameter Tredrea water-wheel (bottom left corner, above) was powered by a leat across the road in the foreground but out of the picture and was used to pump water to supply the villagers. To the right of Cove Hill (the road, centre foreground), on the far side of the white building, is the old mill of the Manor of Arworthal, which originally had a wheel at each end, driven by water from the same leat. On the far side of the road is the entrance to the foundry yard, formerly, as here, by means of a bridge across the Kennal River until road widening took place in 1955, when the old course was filled in and a new course created, flowing diagonally across the yard where a new bridge was built. The building to the right of the entrance was used as management offices, while the weighbridge in the small shed to the left of the entrance and the foundry offices next to it marked the limit of navigation for the shallow-draught lighters

that brought their cargoes to this head of navigation. On the far side of the yard is where the many processes involved in the foundry business were carried on, such as the casting shop with its famous arch (above), one of the few relics that remains of the former foundry. Behind this stood moulding and pattern shops, a forge and, out of the picture to the left, the gasworks, which supplied illumination as well as coke for the furnaces. These operations were first driven by five water-wheels, using a second, higher leat on the far side of the valley, much of which can still be found in place. Water power was used for about seven months of the year but, when the river capacity was reduced in the summer, two steam engines supplied the necessary energy. In the trees on the far side of the valley the smoke denotes the presence of a secluded terrace of workers' cottages, known as Foundry Row (see p. 67), from which paths and steps led down to the rear of the foundry buildings. The close-up picture of the foundry yard (above) shows the machine and fitting shop on the right, moulding and casting shops at the far end and the end of the casting shop at the left. The iron arch (inset, above), dated 1791, is one of three in the original foundry. It is believed to have been cast in one of the South Wales foundries in which the Foxes had business interests, as the first record of casting taking place on this site dates from 1797. Fox business interests moved towards Falmouth Docks in the mid-nineteenth century. The foundry was taken over by the Williams family in 1856 and continued under their management until 1879, employing up to six hundred men producing mining engines, machinery and equipment for Cornish mines, as well as exporting these products to Spain, Mexico, South America and Australia.

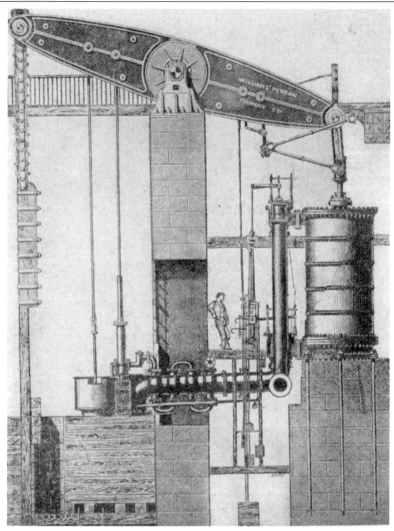

This extract from Williams's Perran foundry catalogue shows one of the largest engines to have been manufactured there. Built for United Mines in 1840, its cylinder was 85 in. in diameter and, when installed, it was used for pumping water from the mines. Known as Taylor's engine, it had a stroke of 11 ft, which pumped 500 gallons of water per minute. When in use on United Mines it would have been in an engine-house, remains of many of which can be seen throughout the mining areas of Cornwall. The engine-man is leaning against the 'bob-wall' of the house, on which the 'beam' or 'bob' is balanced. Everything to the right of the wall would have been inside the house and as the steam engine moved the inside end of the 'bob' up and down, the corresponding movement of the other end moved the 'rod' on the extreme left up and down the shaft to work the pumps. In addition to supplying engines to mines, the foundry sent its pumping equipment to numerous waterworks throughout the country, as well as for the Severn Tunnel and for draining Haarlem Lake in the Netherlands.

After the Williams foundry closed and its workers dispersed, the site was leased by the Edwards family in 1891. The business was managed by two brothers, T.P. and W.H. Edwards, for the combined business of woollen manufacture (by W.H.) and corn and seed merchants (by T.P.). The textile branch was concerned with items manufactured from woollen cloth brought in and prepared for sale – mainly the production of blankets and the preparation of serge cloth for distribution to tailors throughout the West Country. Production lasted until 1911, when competition from Yorkshire mills forced the closure of the company. The corn and agricultural foodstuffs branch expanded and thrived under the management of T.P. Edwards. In this 1893 photograph the millyard is seen with a delivery van, to the right of which is T.P. Edwards, with brother W.H. Edwards behind him. The business was very much a family concern, and of T.P.'s five daughters four married into the business. After his death in 1934, three of his sons-in-law became directors of Edwards Brothers, which carried on with milling and animal foodstuffs manufacture until the company was taken over by J. Bibby and Son in 1969 and the premises were used as a distribution centre for its products in Cornwall. The site now lies derelict with some of the buildings in a dangerous condition.

Among the changes made by the Edwards Brothers in the layout of the mill was the construction of a 'cut' from the river as it flowed under Carclew Bridge to a new three-storey water-mill, driven by an extension to the leat along the south side of the valley. The water-wheel is visible in the picture below, with a derelict barge that had been used to bring grain up to the mill at high tide. By the mid-1920s, however, road transport had taken over completely and the two barges, *Ivy* and *Daisy*, rotted away and eventually sank in the tail-race of the mill. The water-wheel was removed in 1953.

The stream that flows into Perran Creek has been, for its length, probably the most exploited stretch of water in Cornwall. It rises 5½ miles above Perran foundry on the Carnmenellis Moor, just north of Carnkie. Its headstream 'catchment area' is now occupied by the massive Stithians Reservoir, but formerly this was a collecting ground for the water that ran down the valley south of Stithians, where it worked this paper mill at 'Little Plymouth'. The size of the overshot wheel and the adjacent building suggests that this must have been an important local industry, and it is likely to be the 'manufactory for superior quality paper' mentioned in the *Royal Cornwall Gazette* of March 1809. It was the first white-paper mill in Cornwall, which, by 1851, had come under new management producing paper and millboard. In the latter half of the nineteenth century the paper was made from old calico and hessian flour-bags sent from Plymouth. There is no trace of it today. Just below this spot the river plunges steeply down through the wooded Kennel Vale, dropping about 65 yards in just over half a mile through the steep-sided valley.

As a result of the increasing demands of the mining and quarrying industries for explosives at the beginning of the nineteenth century, the Cosawes Wood Gunpowder Factory was established in 1809. It was not long before the Fox family, already established at Perran foundry not far down the valley, realized the commercial benefits of this industry and set up a second manufactory in Kennal Vale, which had the advantages of abundant water power, nearby granite for construction of such massive buildings as that shown here and a damp atmosphere in the wooded valley. By 1844 the venture was so successful that a completely new works was set up in Roches Wood, farther up the valley, thus doubling the capacity of the Kennal Vale Gunpowder Works. By this time the Cosawes site had been taken over and was used for storage only.

This water-wheel is one of the few remaining of what were, as early as 1838, forty-eight wheels along the length of the Kennal River. The complicated arrangement of mills, processing buildings and leats that drove the wheels in the remains of the old gunpowder works may be clearly seen today as a result of the excellent work done in Kennal Vale by the Cornwall Trust for Nature Conservation, the members of which have cleared the site and opened it to the public, having been granted a long lease on the 21 acres of this historic site. Nearer to Ponsanooth village, but associated with gunpowder manufacture, were charcoal mills, a saltpetre refinery (see p. 79), a sulphur mill and a cooper's shop which made barrels for the powder. By 1875 production had reached its peak, but the decline of the Cornish mining industry, combined with the invention of new types of explosive such as dynamite and gelignite, resulted in a gradual reduction in output until their closure in 1910.

At the lower end of the former gunpowder works are the remains of the Lower Gloom Store, with the ruins of its boiler house and granite chimney. This was towards the end of the gunpowder-making process when steam from the boiler was employed to dry the powder. During the ninety-eight years of the company's productive existence there were surprisingly few accidents, although those that did occur were often spectacular and widely reported in the local newspapers. In a 'melancholy accident' in February 1826 a man and woman were killed. The latter had been roasting potatoes away from the mixing house, but carried a spark in on her clothing. In June of that year a man and boy were cleaning out a mill and died from injuries resulting from an explosion, which, at the subsequent enquiry, could not be explained. In June 1838 a 'dreadful explosion' blew up five mills, seriously injuring one man. In January 1841 'an inquest was held on the body, or to speak more correctly, the fragments of the body (for the poor fellow was literally blown to pieces) of John Martin', whose head had been found a quarter of a mile away from the scene of the explosion. As time went on, however, accidents became less frequent as safety regulations became stricter.

The Kennal Vale Company had a warehouse in Penryn, through which raw materials for gunpowder manufacture were imported by sea. One of these constituents was saltpetre, which was refined in this building nearer to Ponsanooth village and away from the danger area. It closed in 1898 when gunpowder manufacture ceased, but was reopened in the 1920s by the Bickford Smith Company of Tuckingmill, makers of safety fuse, for the manufacture of gutta percha, a rubbery material used to provide a waterproof coating for the fuse. It was still in use by the Nobel Explosive Company in the 1960s. These four photographs of the gunpowder works are by H.G. Ordish and are reproduced by permission of the RIC.

These two views of the Magdalen mine, situated just below the Ponsanooth Viaduct (which was replaced by a masonry structure in 1930), show the most recent period of working between 1926 and 1930. Mentioned as early as 1520, the mine has been worked intermittently since then. One of its problems was the presence of magnetite in the ore. This was difficult to separate from the black tin until the invention of the magnetic separator enabled it to be worked after 1913, but the low price of tin brought about its closure, as with many other Cornish mines.

Pill Creek to Tolverne

To the west of Pill Creek stands Porthgwidden, which was built around1830 by Edmund Turner, MP for Truro, at which time the estate ran south to Restronguet Point (see p. 40). From 1842 to 1890 it was the home of the Revd Tom Philpotts, vicar of Feock, which included the growing port of Devoran until a separate parish was created in 1873. In 1961 Porthgwidden was converted into a number of separate accommodation units, but it still occupies a commanding position at the north-west corner of Carrick Roads.

At the extreme northern end of Carrick Roads, east of Porthgwidden, is Loe Beach, not to be confused with Loe Bar, near Helston. In such a position it is not surprising that, in December 1877, with the wind blowing at hurricane force from the south-east, three Truro schooners at anchor in Carrick Roads were driven on to Loe Beach 'as far as the unusually high tide could carry them'. A short distance farther east is one of the smallest of all of the creeks on the estuary, Pill Creek. The picture above shows this southward-looking inlet with eighteen Working Boats at anchor and another against the quay on the east side, against the slipway. This quay, as with so many others, was used to load the produce brought down from the mines on to sailing vessels. There is a story told of the mules carrying powdered arsenic in pannier baskets, which irritated their skin. When turned out into a field above the creek before returning to the mines, the mules would roll on the ground to relieve the irritation and, over the years, nothing would grow in that part of the field as a result of the poison in the soil. The end cottage of the row behind the quay was at one time an inn, and in 1812 a newspaper advertisement for its sale described it as an 'established more than fifty years . . . now has full business which is daily improving from the great increase in the coasting trade'. Below is an opulent pleasure-boat, *L'Oiseau Blessée*, against the quay, with its load of three couples. The boatman is standing on the quay. The railway line leading into the water is something of a mystery and has, so far, defied explanation.

Pill Creek

The commerce of Pill Creek is summed up in these pictures. Above, a topsail schooner lies on the mud against the quay, having unloaded its cargo, perhaps coal, as *Kelly's Directory* of 1893 lists 'John Kellow, coal merchant of Pill Creek'. The surprisingly large number of Working Boats in these pictures suggests that oyster dredging was at one time a very significant occupation. Below, five oystermen have brought ashore their sacks of shellfish from the boats at anchor behind them, or they may have gathered them from the beach. Another local activity was shipbuilding on the shore around the creek. Hitchens and Ford took over Hodge's yard in the late 1860s and built the schooners *Reaper* and *Lizzie Edith*. Working in the yard was a young Pill Creek boy, a shipwright, who was to become something of a legend in the shipyards of the estuary. He was William Ferris, who had by 1867 moved to John Stephens' yard at the entrance to Penpol Creek, later known as Yard Point (see p. 41).

A house has occupied this site for centuries and 'Trelesyk' was mentioned in the Assize Rolls of 1280. The first 'mansion' (above) was built in this superb south-facing position in about 1750 by John Lawrence, whose architect was Edmund Davy, the grandfather of Sir Humphrey Davy, the famous Cornish scientist. In 1790 the estate was bought by Cornwall's richest man, Ralph Allen Daniell, known as 'guinea-a-minute' Daniell on account of the richness of his mining interests. After 1823 his son Thomas made improvements to the property, including the now-famous six-columned portico, looking south across green fields sweeping down to Channals Creek. However, Thomas Daniell's improvements plunged him into debt. After a time he fled to France and the estate came to the Davies Gilbert family in 1844. Carew Davies Gilbert was responsible for laying out the gardens much as they are today. The grounds were used for such parish events as concerts, garden shows, meetings of the Primrose League and temperance societies, at many of which the band of HMS *Ganges* supplied the music. The farms on the estate were greatly improved and modernized, and fish-ponds were created behind Channals Creek. After Daniell's death in 1913, much of the estate was sold, reducing its area from 900 to 300 acres.

Leonard Daneham Cunliffe, a governor of the Bank of England, first rented (1913) then bought (1928) Trelissick (see p. 84). His step-daughter, Mrs Ida Copeland, inherited in 1937 and, with her husband Ronald, was responsible for planting many of the trees and shrubs that make the gardens so beautiful. In 1955 Mrs Copeland gave the house and 376 acres to the National Trust. It is surely the jewel in the crown of National Trust properties in Cornwall today.

Although Trelissick looks out southwards over Carrick Roads, the eastern side of the estate, accessible today as part of the magnificent 'woodland walk', overlooks King Harry Reach. Here, between 1912 and 1932, lay *Implacable* (see *Falmouth*, p. 125, and *Lower Fal*, p. 44), which was brought to the estuary by Mr G.E. Wheatley-Cobb, and used as a training vessel for youth organizations.

The Fal Estuary is known as a 'ria' or drowned valley (see *Lower Fal*, Introduction). One result of this is its deep, central channel winding north through Carrick Roads to Tolverne, which, even at low tide, gives over 32 yards off St Anthony lighthouse and 12 yards at Tolverne, 5 miles from the open sea. This depth of water means that surprisingly large vessels can be taken far up the estuary where they can lie at anchor in perfect safety. A Dutch vessel in its First World War camouflage (above) is seen at anchor against a background of the steeply wooded slopes of King Harry Reach, typical of much of this part of the Fal. The presence of the old wooden sailing ship, *Implacable* (below), with the more modern steel steamship off Trelissick makes an interesting contrast.

Although the sheltered anchorage has been used for centuries, it was between the two world wars that the waterway saw its maximum use when well over a hundred vessels were laid up. During the First World War, as a result of the UK's import requirements and, after 1915, the success of the German submarine offensive, owing to which a number of ships were sunk, many were kept in service long after they should have been scrapped. After the war the great surplus of shipping meant that many had to be broken up or sold overseas, and they were sent to the Fal Estuary to await their fate. The depression of the late 1920s and early 1930s did nothing to alleviate the problem, as these pictures show, and local newspapers kept their readers up to date with arrivals and departures.

The degree of congestion in the upper part of the estuary can be seen in these two pictures, with (above) vessels laid up almost to the shore in the lower part of King Harry Reach and (below) approaching Tolverne Pool, where the junction of several branches of the waterway causes a widening, eight vessels lie abreast off Tolverne with others in the distance in the lower Truro River. Many of the ships here belonged to the Hain Line, the well-known St Ives shipping company, which grew from small beginnings in the mid-nineteenth century and sent ships with characteristic Cornish names all over the world, until it was taken over by P&O and its identity was destroyed in 1972. On the right the River Fal branches off into the most restful part of the whole estuary as it runs up towards Ruan Lanihorne. On the skyline (centre), Tregothnan is clearly visible while below it, at water level, is the estate boathouse (see p. 105).

The riverside house (above) identifies the location as the Malpas end of Tresillian Creek, where, shallow though it was, large ocean-going vessels were laid up after the First World War. It is likely, however, that they lay aground on the mud at low tide. So great was the need for space for laying up ships that several were anchored in such unlikely places as the Penryn River (see *Lower Fal*, p. 118) and off Mylor dockyard (see p. 25).

In the Second World War different types of ship were increasingly seen in the estuary as the demands of war created new varieties of vessels. This trend reached its peak in the 1943–4 build-up for the D-Day invasion of Normandy in June 1944. In this picture, the exact location of which is the subject of some difference of opinion among those who use the estuary, landing craft of the United States Navy lie alongside a jetty, with the inscription of one particular New Englander prominently displayed in the foreground. As the D-Day preparations reached their climax, the estuary became host to more and more of the invasion fleet and every creek was used to house them. New jetties were built and new roads constructed down to the water's edge for loading every type of vehicle from jeeps to heavy tanks. There were embarkation points at Tolverne, Turnaware, Falmouth Docks and Trebah Beach (on the Helford River), and it took a masterpiece of staff work and organization as convoys of vehicles moved gradually towards these points over several days, to be loaded and moved out to form up, awaiting the signal to sail across the English Channel in the largest movement of shipping the world has ever seen. After the initial invasion had taken place, supply vessels plied backwards and forwards across the Channel, and, to quote the words of one member of the crew of Landing Ship Tanks (LST) 266, Edward J. Dyer of Bloomfield, Michigan, 'we made 76 trips across the English Channel starting on D-Day from Falmouth . . . we were one of 34 LST's that loaded out of Falmouth.'

After the Second World War a different scene presented itself in King Harry Reach – that of surplus British warships awaiting their final trip to the breakers yard or sale overseas. HMS *Ajax* (above) lies at anchor. This vessel is famous for its role in the Battle of the River Plate in December 1939, when, in company with HMS *Exeter* and HMS *Achilles*, it engaged the German pocket-battleship *Graf Spee* in an encounter that ended with the German ship being scuttled outside Montevideo. The warships below include HMS *Albatross*, HMS *Cape Town*, HMS *Adventure*, HMS *Caledon* and HMS *Colombo*.

King Harry Passage, named after King Henry VI, to whom a chapel was dedicated in the woods on the eastern side, was crossed by one of the main east to west roads through Cornwall, used by pilgrims en route for St Michael's Mount and more so by Roseland farmers on the way to market. The 'horse-ferry' that developed at this point is shown on the Philleigh side. The broad, flat-bottomed punt-like vessel had hinged planks for loading the carriages and inboard rings for attaching carriages and horses. Below, a ferry is being propelled away from the Feock side, perhaps answering a call from the opposite side. A second ferry is tied against the quay, while a third lies upside-down on the quay, probably undergoing repair. The smaller boat at the bottom of the steps is probably the ferry used for 'passengers only' when no carriages needed to cross.

This picture shows a fully laden ferry unloading on the Feock side. Three gentlemen and their horses have been landed on the beach at low tide (the ferrymen preferred this as the journey was shorter), watched by the almost inevitable clutch of children at the top of the ladder on the quay. Still on the ferry are the three carriages and, seemingly in no hurry to disembark, three ladies. These three photographs, dating from 1870–80, portray the river on a calm day, but crossings were not always as tranquil as these suggest. Newspapers of the time give reports of restless animals taking fright and plunging overboard. On one occasion two horses went in together, taking with them a rider who had been standing between them with the reins wound around his arm. He was rescued by the ferrymen while the horses swam ashore. Other animal freight included sheep, cattle and pigs on the way to Truro Market. Bullocks were made to swim across tied to the side of the ferry, while the smaller animals were landed by throwing them overboard as the ferry approached the landing place. In bad weather a man was often stationed at Turnaware to intercept any animals carried downstream. This method of crossing was unreliable and, as reported in the *West Briton* in February 1887, 'could there not be a better way of crossing the river Fal at King Harry Ferry than has hitherto existed? With a strong south-easterly wind the passage is often impassable and travellers who have come several miles to cross have been obliged to retrace their steps and go round by Truro and Tregony, 20 miles further than they had anticipated. A high level bridge has been suggested by some, a steam ferry by others.' Even after the ferry became mechanized the old horse-boats were kept in reserve and were used up until 1920 when the steam ferry needed to be repaired.

In 1887 the opinions expressed in the newspaper report on p. 93 led to a meeting, chaired by Colonel Tremayne of Carclew, to discuss the formation of a company to operate a steam ferry across King Harry Passage. This proposal met with little support, but a year later, in May 1888, the King Harry Steam Ferry Company Limited was formed with a capital of £2,000. By January 1889, 2,114 shares had been allocated at £1 each, a contract signed for building the ferry and tenders for the necessary shore work advertised. The first ferry, referred to in its early days as a 'ferry bridge', pictured below near the Philleigh side, cost £1,300 and was built by Messrs Sara and Burgess at their works in St Gluvias Creek, Penryn (above). The first crossing was made at 6.00 a.m. on 19 September 1889, with two officials of the company and a newspaper reporter, but later in the day a half-hourly service came into operation and traffic was heavy. Under the heading 'Replacing the horse-boat', the *West Briton* reported: 'The new steam ferry at King Harry Passage is a wonderful accommodation for the district. Carriages are conveyed over every quarter of an hour in about 3¾ minutes . . . the charge for a four-wheeler is 1s. 6d. and other vehicles in proportion.' Throughout its existence the ferry had pulled itself across between the slipways on chains anchored

firmly at each end. For a time the first ferry used a single chain, which made for easier handling and used less coal, but the strain imposed on the single chain meant that it frequently broke, leaving the ferry drifting helplessly. An extra chain was installed and the picture above shows them suspended between the ferry and the shore anchors on the east side. The controllable gate and its safety ramp can be seen, duplicated at the other end, and the engine house and passenger waiting room carries an advertisement for 'Criddle and Co., Wholesale and Retail Furniture'. Also visible are the houses built for ferry personnel at the end of the western slipway and the small self-sufficient settlement of King Harry Passage with its steeply sloping gardens and its quay. The passenger vessel heading towards Truro is the $29\frac{1}{2}$ ton steamer *Truro Belle*, a Rusden-owned vessel built at Dartmouth in 1895 and operated on the Fal for only three years before its sale to a ferry operator in Newcastle. Shareholders in the King Harry Steam Ferry Company earned very little in these early years, as profits were small and outgoings increasingly heavy. In 1890 the Philleigh Causeway had to be rebuilt as it was too steep to handle loaded carts, giving a profit over the year of only £28. However, a year later the profit of £57 enabled a 2 per cent dividend to be paid after £25 went into the reserve fund. The Great Blizzard of 1891 again reduced takings considerably, and it was reported that 'the weather generally had been unfavourable for tourists', although there had been few operational interruptions.

After twenty-four years of operation the first ferry was honourably retired and replaced by a successor of very similar appearance, except that the roof of the engine house was curved. Built by Cox and Co. in Falmouth in 1913, its saving in fuel proved invaluable when the price of coal more than doubled during the First World War, and even more so during the post-war depression when supplies of coal were so difficult to obtain that, at times, wood was burned. In December 1929 the ferry was sunk at her moorings after a collision and repairs took three months. As pleasure travel and tourism increased in the 1930s the company thought seriously about a replacement. In 1934 an old Saltash ferry was bought, but when put into service its operating costs proved far too high as not only did it consume more coal, but an extra crewman had to be employed. After three months the renovated ferry was reinstated on the crossing. The ex-Saltash ferry was sold to a Scottish buyer in 1937, but was wrecked on the north Cornish coast when its tow parted in bad weather. The old ferry continued to operate during the Second World War, when coal supplies once more became a problem as only poor-quality fuel was available. By chance a senior US naval officer, crossing the ferry, was told of the problem and soon afterwards a load of high-quality steam coal was delivered, which continued to the end of the war. The picture above shows the second ferry after the war with naval vessels laid up in King Harry Reach, awaiting disposal. The pictures opposite show different views of the ferry. Above, it is in mid-stream, heading towards the Philleigh side with little traffic on board, while the nearby steamer *St Mawes* awaits a boatload of passengers from the Feock side. Below, the heavily laden ferry takes on a second motor coach on the Feock side, and the long expanse of chain exposed at low tide can be seen.

By 1948 this old ferry was in a very bad state, with its bottom plates nearly worn through. A locally designed replacement was ordered from Holman and Co. of Penzance, but with post-war shortages of both labour and materials the new vessel was not ready until 1951. The old ferry, having sailed the 320 yard Passage for thirty-five years, was sold for £10 (after some scrap merchants had asked £50 to take it away!). But disaster struck as the new ferry was being towed from Penzance. The tow parted in

rough weather, after rounding the Lizard, and the ferry went aground east of Kennack Sands, where it was battered by the waves for several days before it was possible to refloat and tow it to Falmouth Docks. After a costly repair the new ferry was able to start operations in June 1951, in time for the holiday season. The newly designed boat was larger with the bridge and engine house forming a central island, the only one of six ferries on the Passage ever to have this feature. After five years it was decided to convert the propulsion to diesel-electric, but for historic and sentimental reasons the name of the company remained unchanged as the King Harry Steam Ferry Company, a title that persists today. To succeed this ferry, two new, larger vessels have in turn been commissioned to meet the demands made by ever-increasing road traffic since 1960. In 1962 a former Saltash ferry was bought after the construction of the Tamar Road Bridge had made it redundant, and the sixth, and present, ferry was built in 1974 by Dredge and Marine Limited in its small yard at Ponsharden on the Penryn River (see *Lower Fal*, p. 119). A local source of disagreement has long been exactly how many miles is saved by using the King Harry ferry. The answer, naturally, depends on the journey undertaken, but between Falmouth and St Mawes the crossing saves 13½ miles, but also adds novelty and the pleasure of some wonderful scenery to the journey.

These pictures show the popular Tolverne 'Smugglers' Cottage' as it was earlier in the twentieth century, when it was an essential part of the trans-estuary communication system. Passengers are on the slipway beside the ferry boat (above). It is not surprising that such a beautiful part of the waterway has long been popular as a landing place. The picture below refers to the same building as a picnic house. There were two cottages here up until 1928, one of which was occupied by the ferryman who operated the crossing to the Coombe side of the river. He was drowned in an accident on his way home from a visit to the cinema in Truro. In 1934 the Newman family took up residence, and since then they have developed the site as a riverside tea-garden.

TOLVERNE PICNIC HOUSE R. FAL.

As part of preparations for the D-Day invasion of 1944 this jetty was built at Tolverne and used by the US Navy for servicing and loading landing craft. Originally it was T-shaped, but the end was knocked off in the late 1940s by a large (non-local) tug, towing away one of the ships laid up in the Fal. The whole structure was removed some time later. To give easier access by land to this otherwise remote spot, a new road and slipway were built by civilian workers, who did the same at Turnaware at the southern end of King Harry Reach. Like Tolverne, this was one of the major embarkation points for the D-Day operation. The cottages (opposite page) were taken over by the Admiralty. Ten rooms were used as offices and accommodation by US naval staff, who had thirteen telephones installed. The Newman family continued to live in the rear of the building. Mr Rodney Newman was employed ferrying workers and carrying materials for road and slipway building, in addition to towing the decoy landing craft, made of canvas and wood in nearby creeks, to various parts of the estuary. To deceive enemy reconnaissance aircraft, decoy towns were laid out alongside the Ruan and Tresillian Creeks. In April 1941 a German air attack succeeded in sinking a French naval vessel, *La Suipe*, off Tregothnan Woods, and considerable bravery was shown in rescuing the crew. The boat's skeletal remains are still visible at low tide. Local civilian volunteers regularly patrolled the upper part of the estuary between 1940 and 1944 (see pp. 134–6).

This part of the estuary is on the west side, opposite Tolverne and branching from the northern end of King Harry Reach. To the left is the small unspoilt Lamouth Creek, along the southern shore of which runs the lovely Trelissick woodland walk. To the right the larger Cowlands Creek stretches over half a mile to the bridge at Cowlands, on the northern shore of which is the small village of Coombe, the centre of a very fertile agricultural area (see p. 104). The wooded promontory between the creeks is Roundwood, renowned equally for its prehistoric fort as for its quay (above). The Iron Age earthworks are believed to date from about 350 BC and consist of an oval enclosure, 125 × 50 yards, which has never been properly excavated. The reason for its site is something of a mystery, and the suggestion that it was meant to guard the confluence of creeks does not stand up to serious investigation. The quay, dating from the seventeenth century, was one of several on the estuary originally constructed for the export of copper and tin ore from the mines in its western hinterland. Traffic declined in the nineteenth century as a result of the construction of the railway to Devoran, but, unlike many other quays that fell into disuse, this one received a second lease of life when it was taken over by Henry Trethowan, the renowned shipbuilder at the Little Falmouth yard. He not only built boats there but finished off those started on Penryn River, such as the *Flora of Penryn*, a 109 ton cattle trader.

These pictures portray Cowlands (sometimes referred to as Cowlings) Creek. Above, a closer view on one of Bragg's 'Peeps of the Fal' postcards shows the *Princess Victoria* steaming down river past Roundwood Quay, with the sheds built by Henry Trethowan for his shipbuilding operations. In the trees towards the back of the quay are traces of the old saw-pit, used by the sawyer and his apprentice to cut the timber for the boats, such as the barge *Ellen*, which was built for bargeman William Burley of Newham in 1874. Early in the twentieth century Scoble's coalyard occupied the quay. Later the same family ran a boat-hire business and tea-garden up until the Second World War. Today the quay and the surrounding area are looked after by the National Trust as a pleasant picnic and recreation area. The high tide view (below) looks farther up the creek, where one of Trethowan's workmen, Wellington, set up a yard of his own near Cowland's Farm where he built two schooners: *WRT* and *William John*.

The small waterside village of Coombe was renowned in the past for its orchards or 'gardens' of the black, damson-liked Kea plums, which were sent to markets in Truro and other towns in the west of the county. The *West Briton* of October 1890 reported that 'a total of 20 acres is divided into holdings between ¼ and 3 acres . . . produce a beautiful blossom in spring (when boatmen organise trips to see the "plum gardens") and a harvest in August/September. Picking and packing goes on from 8.00 a.m. to dusk and trees overhanging the creek are shaken into boats at high tide. The fruit is sorted and counted in sheds along the shore and packed into baskets lined with ferns or dry grass, but not straw as this gives the fruit a musty flavour.' Another activity around the creek was 'barking', which involved removing the bark from oak trees so that it could be sent to tanneries in Truro. The picture of Coombe below illustrates how dependent the local people used to be on water transport – not only for shopping in Truro but for fetching coal from Roundwood Quay and milk from Roundwood Farm.

Up to Tregony

Little remains today of this attractive thatched Tregothnan boathouse near the junction of Truro River and Ruan Creek. Having fallen into disrepair, much of its stone has been removed for use elsewhere. In the past Lord Falmouth allowed its upper rooms to be used by members of Truro Corporation, who had performed the ceremony of 'beating the bounds' of the Borough (see *Lower Fal*, p. 2). The boats were kept in the lower part of the house where they were afloat at high tide.

The old Plantagenet house that stood on this site was sacked during the Civil War and the only trace of it today is at the entrance to the kitchen garden. Although the present house dates from 1652, this was largely rebuilt and considerably enlarged in 1811 as the magnificent Tregothnan House. The estate came into the Boscawen family by marriage in 1334. In the early eighteenth century Hugh Boscawen became the first Lord Falmouth, but the most famous member of the family was Edward, brother of the second viscount, who, in a distinguished naval career, when he was known as 'Old Dreadnought', became one of the Lords of the Admiralty in 1751 at the early age of forty. The cannons on the terrace at Tregothnan came from his house in London and the Adam Memorial to him is in the estate church at nearby St Michael Penkevil. The gardens have been lovingly nurtured by several generations of the family, and well repay a visit on those occasions when the present viscount opens them to the public for charity. The estate, which is bounded on three sides by the waters of the Truro River and the Ruan and Tresillian Creeks, has a deer park at the southern end, overlooking the Fal. Royalty have often been entertained here when visiting the county, especially for the ceremonies involving Truro Cathedral, but hospitality has also been bestowed on local organizations, as the *West Briton* of June 1849 reported, when 130 members of Falmouth Athenaeum Club were taken up river by the tug *Sydney*, normally in use on Restronguet Creek. The weather was fine, Falmouth band played and, after landing at two o'clock, 'proceeded to inspect the grounds, gardens and castle, the domestics having received instructions to afford the visitors every facility for doing so. They afterwards sat down, some on the lawn, others in the boathouse, to a splendid cold collation . . . hams, tongues, chicken pies, roast ducks, Cornish pasties . . . After dinner the whole party enjoyed themselves with a variety of dancing, polkas, waltzes, quadrilles, country dances . . . until about five o'clock when the ladies commenced tea: . . . all passed off with admirable order and about ten o'clock the company returned to the society's reading room where the devoted lovers of Terpsichore kept up their amusements until a late hour.'

The unspoilt and rarely visited Ruan Creek is without doubt the loveliest part of the whole estuary, and its beauty can be appreciated best from a boat, as few roads and footpaths reach its shores. The creek penetrates deeply into the northern part of the fertile Roseland Peninsula. Evidence of other occupations in the past exists in Tuckingmill Creek, suggesting an association with a branch of the textile industry, and the square chimney-stack of the Trelonk brickworks, whose employees are shown here, in the fields below Trelonk Farm, bordering the river. One of several brickworks around the estuary, it is said to have used the river silt, rich in china clay, as its raw material up until its closure in 1907. *Kelly's Directory* of 1893 lists it as the 'Trelonk Brick and China Clay Company'.

On a small tributary creek, about 440 yards east of the Fal Valley as it stretches north towards Tregony, stands the small village of Ruan Lanihorne, one of the most peaceful spots on the estuary. Life in the early twentieth century is depicted here, when the remoteness of the village made transport on the river that lapped its shores a vital part of life, especially as the water was then deep enough for easy access by small boats. The picture below, looking in the opposite direction towards the Fal, shows the ingenious way in which a boat under repair was supported by a makeshift tripod.

Life in the upper estuary is shown here in two pictures of the turn of the century. Above, two men are fishing for flatfish in the shallow water at low tide, as evidenced by the wide expanse of mud behind them. Exactly how they are doing this is uncertain, as is the function of the tall poles projecting from the mud. Are these part of the fishing operation or do they mark the deep channel, to be used by boatmen when the tide is high? The picture below is more straightforward, with the trading barge *Eclipse* lying high and dry on the mud below the village. As late as the 1930s vessels such as this were carrying cargoes of coal, grain, roadstone and fertilizer to this point.

These pictures show the King's Head at Ruan Lanihorne. The thatched inn above, with the customary band of interested villagers, was burned down in 1898 and replaced by the building below, behind the pony and trap. Visiting this peaceful spot today it is difficult to imagine that up until the sixteenth century it had a large castle with eight towers, said to have been second only to Launceston, although the reason for building such an edifice here remains something of a mystery. There was, according to Charles Henderson, the eminent Cornish historian, no village at that time, the nearest settlement being at Sheepstall, halfway up the

valley towards Tregony, with a market and St Margaret's leper hospital. An interesting history of the area, written in 1791 by the Revd John Whitaker, relates that the castle stretched from the water's edge well up the hillside to the east of the church. Boazio's map of 1597 (see pp. 6 & 7) names the castle, although it had been unoccupied since the 1530s and the stone was being used to build the cottages in the expanding village. Whitaker suggests that the castle must have supported a sizeable garrison as it contained a brewhouse and a coalyard, with a dock cut from the creek reaching up to the walls where there was probably a watergate. After its demolition the castle well was taken over by the village, and traces of it can still be seen. The Cornish historian Tonkin, writing in the 1730s, said that only one of the towers was left standing, yet Borlase in his *Antiquities* of 1769 does not mention it, suggesting that the castle had disappeared by then. Navigation in the upper reaches of the estuary has become increasingly difficult as a result of sedimentation, brought about by the 'streamworks' of the tinners farther upstream. Barges were encouraged to dredge the sand away with the offer of 1s. a load. By 1791 barges were unable to reach the village, but, even then, coal vessels had to unload at Kiln Point below the village. With the advent of china clay extraction farther upstream, sedimentation grew worse and navigable tidal water became shallower. Today, only at a high spring tide does water of any depth approach the village, which is separated from the deeper tidal water by expanses of saltmarsh, through which the Ruan River runs, in a trench, up to 6 ft deep. Transport for the inhabitants was considerably eased in the early years of the twentieth century when Mr W.S. Blamey bought one of the lifeboats from the wrecked liner *Mohegan*, installed a steam engine and operated the ferry (above) up until 1914. It travelled between Ruan Lanihorne, Tolverne and Truro, every Wednesday and Saturday. Mr Blamey, standing beside the funnel, was a very obliging ferryman as he was prepared to do shopping in Truro for those unable to make the journey themselves.

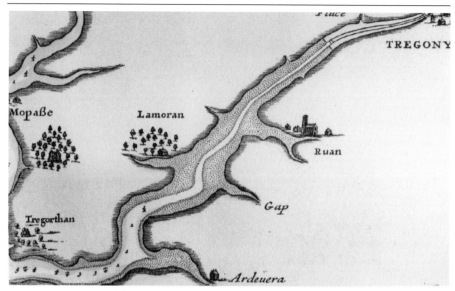

Tregony was an important port in the Middle Ages. First tin streaming, then china clay extraction in the Fal Valley above the town, resulted in severe silting, so that when Tregony Bridge was built in about 1300 it replaced Grampound as the lowest crossing point of the river. This section of the Greenville Collins map of 1693 shows some sort of reclamation work below the town, possibly that of about 1680 by Charles Trevanion, who built locks and sluices to allow boats to reach farther upstream. However, all was in vain and eventually Sett Bridge was built even lower down, near Ruan Lanihorne, as the lowest crossing point, which it remains today. At Nansaker Mill the roof of a building barely projects above the present valley floor, indicative of the depth of sediment.

The Gregor Arms stands as a private house today on the west side of the bridge. Its name derives from the one-time lords of the manor of Trewarthenick, a mile to the south-west. The delightful old steam lorry of T. Rowse of Probus has solid iron wheels and appears to be loaded with bags of flour.

As with Ruan Lanihorne, Tregony once boasted a castle, which was situated just above the present bridge, but no trace of it remains. The borough returned two members to Parliament, one of several Cornish 'rotten' boroughs to do so, up until 1832, before which it had earned for itself a notoriety for bribery and menaces at election time. Much of the land in the district was owned by the Boscawen family. In 1696 Hugh Boscawen bequeathed a charity fund for six 'decayed housekeepers', as a result of which these almshouses were built. Having been restored in 1895, they are still occupied today.

After its demise as a port, Tregony remained an important market town, especially for wool. The once extensive market house stood at the top of the main street, but as the woollen trade declined the building became ruinous. It was demolished and its site marked by the clock tower, which was erected in 1833. In this early twentieth-century view the earth road is bordered on each side by stone-lined gutters to carry away the water on the steep slope. The horsedrawn carrier's cart has probably brought goods from the nearest railway station at Grampound Road, over 3 miles to the north. A walk along the town's main street today shows that the arrangement of doors, windows and arches has changed little.

An occupant of Tolverne Cottage after 1934, Mr Rodney Newman was an inveterate explorer of the upper reaches of the Fal. In September 1956 he had become what the *Western Morning News* described as 'the first man to take a powered boat up the River Fal from Sett Bridge to Tregony Bridge'. Here, in March 1958, in the company of his son, George (in the boat), and Barry Richards, Mr Newman is standing on the river bank. He took 'his pioneering venture a stage further by taking his boat . . . from Tregony Bridge to Fal Bridge at Grampound, a distance of four miles'. The newspaper then went on to describe the exploit: 'the boat was brought overland to Tregony Bridge . . . where the three men boarded her' (above). At that point there was about 5 ft of water – the river is not tidal at Grampound. Mr Newman said: 'The first half mile went well but then we hit a rock which broke the propeller spring but I had come prepared with spare springs and we fitted a new one. The farther upstream we went, the faster were the down-currents and on the twists of the river we had all we could do to make headway. On passing under Golden Mill Bridge we struck another rock breaking another spring. We then had to pull the dinghy up about 50 yards over the rocks. About half a mile from Golden Mill we nearly capsized when we hit a tree stump. At one point we had to hitch a rope around a tree and haul the dinghy up several yards. When we got 100 yards from Grampound Bridge we hit another large rock.' Mr W.L. Dunn, a garage proprietor who lived adjacent to the Fal Bridge, said he had been at Grampound for fifty-two years and had never known a boat to come up there.

SECTION SIX

To Malpas and Tresillian

This bend in the river is at Woodbury Corner, named after the large white house on the left shore. The quay in the right foreground, with its characteristic dry-stone construction, has now almost completely disappeared. Originally it stood on the north side of Parson's Creek, nearly opposite Kea Old Church (see p. 116). The large topsail schooner beyond the end of the quay has brought a cargo, probably of timber, to be unloaded in that part of the river, between Church Creek and Malpas, known as Maggotty Bank. Woodbury is associated with Henry Martyn (1781–1812), the local boy who became a great scholar, missionary and saint. The beautiful baptistry in Truro Cathedral, with its superb collection of Cornish stones, is dedicated to him.

Some Cornish parishes have no village of the same name. Kea, on the western shore of the estuary above Tolverne Pool, is one of these. The original parish was very large and stretched as far west as Scorrier and Chacewater, which meant that some of the congregation had to make a round journey of 10 miles for each church visit. A new church was built near Killiow, just west of the Falmouth to Truro road, in 1802, but it was so badly built that it had to be replaced by the present church, which is on almost the same site. It was built about 1895 and retains the font, pulpit and three bells from the original church. Only the tower of the first church, a prominent river landmark, which was struck by lightning in the 1890s, is left standing today. It is situated in a garden full of colour in spring with snowdrops, primroses and daffodils, adjacent to the Mission church, on the site of the old Poor House.

This is Malpas Passage at the junction of Tresillian Creek and the Truro River, with the ferry house at the water's edge and the Ship Inn to its left, at one time the only buildings at this point. Part of the Tregothnan estate, the road ran down on the St Michael Penkevil side to the ferry, which once crossed to both St Clement (foreground) and Kea (right, off the picture) shores. Below is the ferry-boat, similar to that at King Harry Passage which operated up until the 1920s. The inn and ferry were leased together and date from the late eighteenth century. This association is not uncommon, since waiting for the ferry can be spent more comfortably inside than out. One of the former tenants was the well-known local lady, Jenny Mopus (really, Jane Davis), who operated the ferry for some time in the early nineteenth century. In about 1850 the inn closed and its name was transferred to the village across the water. There another hostelry was established, where a jetty was built to give easier access from the water in 1863. This Ship Inn closed in the early 1920s.

Surprisingly large vessels were able to reach Malpas to unload cargo for Truro. In these pictures, typical of the seaborne activity of the early twentieth century, two barquentines with lighters alongside (above) and three topsail schooners (below) lie at anchor. Looking at this stretch of water today it is not easy to visualize such trade, but in March 1873 the *West Briton* reported that in ten days 43 vessels had unloaded at Malpas: 20 coasters, mostly with coal, 16 Norwegian ships with timber, 6 French vessels with grain and 1 three-masted schooner from Iquique with guano.

This more recent scene in Woodbury Reach, with the woods of St Michael Penkevil forming a luxuriant backdrop, shows the steamer *Sophie* at anchor, discharging cargo into lighters, with the *New Resolute* steaming by as it plies its alternative, out-of-season, trade as a tug (see p. 120). In September 1838 a most unusual company was formed to fish in these waters: the Truro Porpoise Fishing Company. This was to operate in the Fal Estuary, aiming to catch twelve porpoises a day. A large tank was to be built at Malpas and before the end of the year 90,000 gallons of oil, to the value of £23,000, were to be produced. However, by December the sale by auction of the 'sean net' was advertised. Described as 'quite new, never having been used . . . 60 fathoms long and twenty feet deep', it was suggested that it could be cut into strips and used by farmers for penning sheep or dividing fields. Also in these waters in 1839, a schooner, *Marie Victoire*, was unloading coal when a Customs officer 'commenced boring in different parts of the vessel and at length sent his gimlet into a cask of brandy', by which time the crew had mysteriously disappeared. The schooner was taken to Truro, where 276 tubs of brandy and geneva were discovered. Then, as was the custom, the vessel was cut up.

This peaceful picture of Malpas, viewed from the ferry house shore, shows the development of the village along its only road, with an expanse of allotment gardens for cultivation by the inhabitants on the south-facing slope behind the houses.

The *New Resolute* passenger tug is proceeding upstream at full steam, early in the twentieth century, with the customary manned attendant boat in tow. The vessel is obscuring one of the village's most important industries – the shipyard of Messrs Scoble and Davies, on the narrow beach below the chapel. Here were built not only *New Resolute*, in 1882, but other vessels such as *Malpas Belle*, a three-masted barquentine for Orchard of Truro, and *Village Bell* and *Janie* for Hitchens and Co. of Truro. All of them were deep-water vessels that frequently sailed a triangular voyage with general cargo to Newfoundland, fish to South America and hides back to Europe.

Here the well-laden passenger tug, *Princess Victoria*, built by Cox and Co. at Falmouth in 1907, is performing both tasks simultaneously as it steams upstream past Malpas on the high tide. The loaded three-masted topsail schooner under tow is probably *Mary Barrow* (see p. 152), on its way to Truro to discharge cargo.

At low tide, passengers had to disembark into rowing-boats to be landed at the Malpas ferry slip and taken on to Truro by road. This passenger vessel is *New Resolute*. In the background are the ferry house, partly obscured by smoke from the funnel, the former Ship Inn and the road leading down to the foreshore. The two white posts below the ferry house indicate the position of the ferry landing site on the St Michael Penkevil side, much of which would have been submerged at high tide.

In more recent time passengers landing at Malpas do not seem to have been subjected to the exertion of clambering into a rowing-boat in mid-stream (see p. 121).
Disembarkation was by means of a permanent landing-stage, here being used by two Newman boats, *Skylark* and *Skylark of Tolverne*. Both of these vessels regularly plied the river with passengers from Falmouth, up until 1961.

Although not really an 'old' photograph, this picture had to be included because it is unique. RMS *Scillonian* is at Malpas on its annual coastal and river excursion from Penzance, but with a blue hull, only seen in 1992. This is certainly the largest vessel to reach Malpas in recent times. This picture is reproduced by permission of Calvin Kneebone, the landlord of the Heron Inn, whose hostelry can be seen above the vessel's stern.

The estuary divides at Malpas, and the oft-used western branch leads to Truro while the eastern creek, hardly used today except by pleasure craft, runs up to Tresillian, the farthest northern point of the waterway, 10 miles from the open sea. Shallow though its upper reaches are today, it, too, was used for river traffic at high tide up until fifty years ago. One of the principal cargoes carried up here – and all over the estuary – up to the latter years of the nineteenth century was limestone. The ruins of what may have been a limekiln remain here, just below St Clement on the Tregothnan shore. Landing on the beach, having rowed across from St Clement, is Margaret Roper Moor. This picture, together with those on the next page, are reproduced by permission of Mrs Moor of St Clement Churchtown. Until replaced by conveniently bagged chemical fertilizers, lime was used widely by farmers on Cornwall's acid soils, in addition to local sea-sand dredged from the river bed. Limestone was imported, usually from Plymouth quarries along the south Cornish coast and from South Wales by north coast ports. Estuaries such as the Fal enabled the 'outside' barges to carry the limestone well inland for offloading directly into kilns built on the water's edge. Remains or records of about forty kilns have been found around the shores of the Fal Estuary. The limestone was laid down with alternate layers of fuel – gorse, bracken, faggots, culm or small coal – and burned to make it more easily soluble before being spread on the fields. In 1843 it was reported that for twenty years, thirty vessels had been employed carrying limestone from Plymouth to south Cornish ports. Accidents often happened when workers fell into a kiln that was fed from its open top. Some unfortunates were overcome by fumes, and most commonly, vagrants, who slept on top of the kilns for warmth on winter nights, were asphyxiated or burned to death.

This old cottage, long replaced by modern housing, was in St Clement and shows the typical working-class rural dwelling of plastered cob wall, thatched roof and single brick chimney. Mr Stephens is busily tending the garden wearing his bowler hat, which seemed to be the standard working headgear. The profusion of bird-boxes attached to the unplastered cob wall presents something of a mystery – they may have been intended to house pigeons, which were often kept for food in winter.

Down on the creekside the young lady is in her canoe, while Canon Alex Page Moor (left) watches as three workmen in the large punt pause in their task of loading floating timber. Along the densely wooded banks of the Upper Fal Estuary, wood was cut and gathered during the summer months and used for fencing, building and winter fuel.

St Clement is a large parish, extending as far west as the outskirts of Truro, but the only settlement of that name is St Clement Churchtown. Originally known as Moresk, after the manor in which it stood, the church probably dates from the twelfth century, but an almost total restoration in 1865 gave it its present appearance. The charming picture of children outside the cottages, the two boys having fetched water from the well, also shows the Ship Inn with its name board over the door. The view below is of the rear of the same thatched hostelry, the name of which suggests that it was used mainly by the crews of the lighters and barges that plied Tresillian Creek. The inn eventually closed in the early years of the twentieth century.

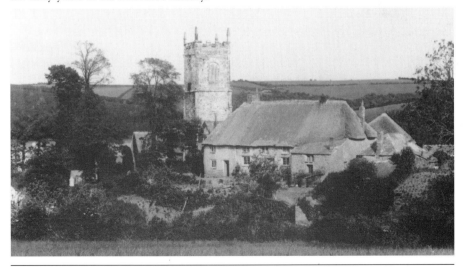

Looking at the creek at St Clement at low tide today it is difficult to believe that waterborne traffic was ever of any importance, but the name of the old inn, together with pictures like this, indicates that it was a significant activity at one time. A sailing barge is discharging cargo, probably coal, into a horsedrawn cart. The tracks in the mud and the fact that the man inside the barge is standing on the cargo shows that unloading is nearly complete. The plank projecting over the starboard bow would have been used when unloading against a quay (see p. 129). Perhaps the bargemen are looking forward to spending the time waiting in the Ship Inn for the tide to rise. Two reasons have been suggested for the closure of the inn, both involving the landowner, Mr Harcourt Williams of Pencalenick (see p. 127). An annual 'rent court' used to be held at the inn, where Mr Williams provided his tenants, once they had paid up, with dinner at a price agreed with the landlord. One year, when he thought he had been overcharged, he gave the landlord notice and let the building as a farm. The second suggestion is that whenever Mr Williams called on a certain tenant, his wife would say he was 'down at the sheep'. However, since he could never find the farmer tending his flock, he became convinced that he was 'at the Ship' and thus he closed the inn.

In this high-tide view of the upper part of Tresillian Creek, St Clement Churchtown is off the picture to the left. The extent of tidal coverage may be seen by comparing this view with that opposite. The large house in the centre, looking south over the creek, is Pencalenick. It was built in 1883 by Michael Henry Williams, whose family occupied the building until the Second World War, when it was requisitioned by the Army and then by American troops. Finally it was used to house Italian prisoners of war. In the late 1940s the house was purchased by the County Council.

The walk along the creekside road between St Clement and Tresillian passes three 'ponds' – originally small creeks but now dammed off from tidal water – at Tresemple, Pencalenick and Kiggon. These were probably created by the landowners for fishing and to encourage birds for wildfowling. Another such feature, Merther Pond, can be found on the Tregothnan side of the creek, between Malpas and St Clement. In this view, Tresemple Pond has frozen over in early 1917 and the local people are taking advantage of this unusual event in various ways.

Despite the shallowing of the creek above St Clement, in the past navigation was possible for barges. Above, two barges are making their way upstream on the tide towards Tresillian, but with sails furled. The larger one in front is motoring, while towing the smaller vessel. It could be a windless day – as the smoothness of the water suggests – or the tide may have begun to drop. Speed up to the head of the creek is essential to avoid stranding. Whatever the reason, the narrowness of the creek, the meandering nature of the deep channel and the vagaries of the wind in such a sheltered creek must have made sailing very difficult. Below, two barges have reached Tresillian – one is afloat while the other rests on the mud. Cargoes carried by vessels like these included coal, timber, grain, roadstone, limestone and building materials.

V 82 Tresillian River

TRESILLIAN.

In these pictures unloading is taking place in the lower part of Tresillian. The workmen pause for the photographer (above) – a welcome rest from the arduous task of unloading from a well-laden barge into one cart, while another waits its turn. Through the trees on the left is the malthouse, where barley was dried for producing malt.

Originally owned by W. and E.C. Carne, brewers of Falmouth and Truro, its workers were allowed six pints of beer a day, free! Below, a different technique of unloading onto the quay is evident. Roadstone is being moved from *Shamrock*, built at Stonehouse, Plymouth, in 1899, by a team of men, usually three in number. The man in the boat (out of sight) loads the basket, a second hauls the basket to quay level and the third, precariously balanced on the plank, empties the basket into the wheelbarrow and tips it on to the quay to enlarge the pile of stone. Here, another man with a second wheelbarrow stands by to speed the process, using the structure on the quayside, which lifts the plank above the pile of stone. This cargo, probably from the quarries on the Lizard, was the last to be carried up to Tresillian by *Shamrock*, which has been superbly rebuilt and is preserved by the National Trust at Cotehele on the River Tamar.

Not only commercial vessels plied to the head of this beautiful creek. On the few occasions that the tide was suitable during the day, *Queen of the Fal* carried passengers up to Gatley's Quay on what this poster, printed for the River Fal Steamship Company, calls 'the most popular trip . . . with passengers . . . landing for one hour (without boats) giving time for tea and to view the beautiful Gothic lodge at the entrance to Lord Falmouth's estate'. As many as three hundred people would travel up on a fine day, and the village cottages did a roaring trade dispensing cream teas. The Bone family set up a business importing timber, coal and lime, at what is now the group of houses called Bone's Cellars Row. When, after 1820, John Gatley took over the business, the quay took his name. He also built ships there, including *Polsue*, which was used as an emigrant ship to North America.

The popular roadside Wheel Inn, seen here taking delivery of a cartload of barrels in the early 1900s, is the sole remaining hostelry of five from the last century. The others were the Ship Inn, closed in 1874, the Blacksmith's Arms, just out of the village at the St Mawes road junction, closed in the 1850s, and two beerhouses in Bone's Cellars Row, behind Gatley's Quay, which were licensed to open for 18 hours a day to serve bargemen and shipbuilders. The cottages on the right have long been demolished in the interests of road widening on this very busy highway. The Wheel Inn was for many years part of the Manor of Polsue, and 'Barton Courts', where tenants paid their rent, were held there. This inn became the 'local' for navvies employed in building the nearby Cornwall Railway in the mid-nineteenth century. Some of them stayed after the railway was completed, their descendants still living in the village.

Although the cottages have been demolished, the turnpike house (left), stands boarded up beside the road as the sole reminder of the early roads built by the Truro Turnpike Trust in 1829. 'Gates' were often sold by auction, and in 1834 this one was sold for £900, the rates for road users having been fixed at: 'Carriages, 6"–9" wheel, 3d. per wheel; 4½"–6", 4d. per wheel; less than 4½", 8d. per wheel; droves of oxen, cows etc., 10d. per score; every donkey, 1d.' The difference in charges for varied wheel sizes was aimed at discouraging narrow wheels, which badly damaged the road surface.

As with most creek-head villages, settlement was preceded by the building of a bridge. Here the location was originally called 'Tresillian Bridge', and was named as such in the document signed by Lord Hopton on the surrender of Royalist forces in Cornwall to General Fairfax in 1646. Dated 1535, the bridge was taken over by the Turnpike Trust in 1754. In 1826 that organization built the present road along the creekside to Truro. The road includes the infamous Woodcock Corner, south of the village, named after a favourite horse of Lord Falmouth, which collapsed and died there. Turnpike trusts were dissolved in 1874 when roads were taken over by County Councils. Several road widenings have taken place since then to cope with the ever-increasing volume of traffic through the village.

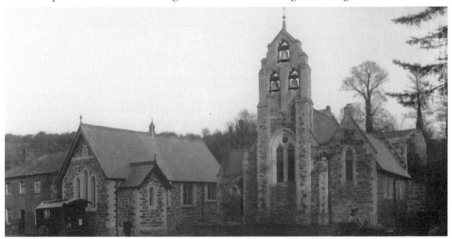

Holy Trinity church, which stands alone in the view above, was established as a mission church in 1878 and became a parish church in 1904, as Tresillian prospered at the expense of Merther, from where two bells, a pulpit, a font and plate were moved to Tresillian. The school (left), with the church missionary wagon parked outside, was opened in October 1905. School records of the early days show how times have changed. Before fires were installed, many children were absent with illness because the school was cold. The 'earth closets' in the yard (called 'offices' in the report) were said to smell offensive as not enough dry earth was available. Some children were unable to attend at a high tide when the road was under water. As road traffic increased in the 1930s the absence of a footpath was said to be a danger in 1936. In June 1944 the school closed for several days, because of the volume of traffic carrying American troops and supplies moving to the embarkation points in preparation for the D-Day invasion of Europe.

This rural scene was recorded before 1904, as the church tower (opposite) had not been built to replace the small spire, which is visible here. The road in the centre curves away into the rich agricultural land of the north Roseland towards Merther and St Michael Penkevil, while, to the right, the ornate private gateway (below) to the Tregothnan estate gives access to the 4 miles of creekside road leading to Tregothnan House (see p. 106).

In July 1940, after the fall of France and when invasion threatened Britain, the Local Defence Volunteers were formed, a name changed later to Home Guard. The Truro River Patrol was formed to look after the upper part of the estuary as far south as Turnaware. Above, the unit is being inspected by its commanding officer, Captain R. Bennett Webb (with the beard) on the beach at Malpas. Although similar waterborne units are known to have been formed on the Upper Thames and on Lake Windermere, where the main task was to prevent enemy seaplanes from landing, Truro members wore distinctive badges and the River Patrol is believed to have been the only Home Guard unit to have worn a navy blue uniform, although some are wearing khaki here. Patrols began in August 1940 and continued until 1944. The boats used were owned by members of the patrol. Initially there were five vessels, but two more were added when weather conditions showed that cabin boats were sometimes needed. No maintenance grants were made for the use of the boats until 1942. Truro City Corporation provided a room at Malpas as a local headquarters, in addition to a garage for the car used when boats could not leave from Truro because of the tide. Farther down river Mr Rodney Newman loaned a room free of charge so that men on duty could get a few hours sleep. All members of the unit had to work during the day, of course. Later in the war this facility was moved to Lime Quay, on the shore below Tregothnan. The river was patrolled every night, irrespective of weather conditions, to enforce the regulations governing immobilization of boats and keeping unauthorized boats off the river during prohibited hours. The men also provided communications across the river when the ferries were not running, especially for army despatch riders, also assisting other Home Guard units in their operations and training.

Brigadier Croft is seen here with members of his staff and senior members of the River Patrol, shortly after the unit had been inspected. To the left of the brigadier stand Captain Bennett Webb (who, by day, had a draper's shop in Truro) and his son David, aged thirteen, and a regular, if unofficial, member of the River Patrol. It is he who has been kind enough to supply the pictures and information on these pages. Below, several of the boats used by the River Patrol are assembled during an exercise at Malpas, including Rodney Newman's *Lizard*, an old pulling lifeboat (extreme left) and Captain Webb's *Mistral* (far right).

Training facilities and equipment for the River Patrol were provided by the Navy and RAF, including a Hotchkiss machine-gun, which was mounted on the bow of *Mistral* (above). In addition to the nightly patrol's normal duties, other work included extinguishing fires carelessly left burning by farmers and assisting the Royal Navy on various duties in the upper estuary. When the French sloop *La Suipe* was sunk above Tolverne in April 1941, the River Patrol was commended for its work in reporting the incident promptly and for rendering assistance. Training for members included communications, such as Morse signalling, as below, where signals are being sent between Lime Quay and *Mistral*, first aid, weapon training and drill.

The Port of Truro

Another village that grew up around a creek-head bridge is Calenick, half a mile south of Truro on the coach road to Falmouth. The stream flowing under the bridge, behind the cart, empties into a creek off to the right. It rises near Chacewater, 4½ miles to the west, and its course passes through an intensively mined area, which has resulted in severe silting problems. In addition to the tin smelting works, seen here across the bridge, there was, after 1770, an industry making crucibles from china clay, brought in from Grampound, which were used in assaying and smelting.

The chimney-stack and clock tower show the location of the Calenick smelting works. After the invention of the reverberatory furnace, in which cheap coal was used instead of charcoal, the earliest of these works was set up at Newham in 1705 at the mouth of Calenick Creek. Production moved to Calenick in 1711, and under several owners – Lemon, Daniell, Michell and Bolitho – tin was smelted for 180 years until the closure of the works in 1891. By 1794 it had ten furnaces in operation and by 1815 it was the county's second largest producer of metallic tin, after Angarrack, near Hayle. In its time it took black tin from nearly fifty different mines in central and west Cornwall, but by 1891 it had become old and inefficient. In November 1892 the *West Briton* carried a notice of its sale: 'comprising clock tower and sheds, smelting house, smithy, bar tin house, culm house, brick house and loft, dressing floor, shed and buddles, four-stall stable and loft over . . . also the crucible works . . . comprising workshops, pug mill (worked by water power), kiln, drying room, stock room, stores, yard and premises now in the occupation of Messrs F. Michell and Co. as yearly tenants at the annual rent of £10. Access to these premises by road and rail (a special siding being within 300 yards) and the river provides access by water.' Other smelting houses were established in Truro during the nineteenth century, not only because of its port facilities but also because it was one of the county's coinage towns, where tin sales took place twice a year until 1838, when the costly and time-wasting ceremony of coinage, together with its many abuses, was abolished. There were three other smelting houses in Truro. Carvedras was established in about the middle of the eighteenth century and reached peak production after 1792, when it was acquired by the Daubuz family. By 1849 it had become the most productive of the eleven works in Cornwall. In 1891 it was amalgamated with Calenick, Trereife and Chyandour (the latter two in the Penzance area) as the Consolidated Tin Smelting Company, but it was closed after seven more years. The Truro Smelting Works was built in 1816 near the head of the navigation of the River Allen, near Trafalgar Wharf. It had a somewhat chequered history under several owners until it closed in 1871. The premises were taken over by a wholesale grocer, although the works' characteristic square stack survived until about 1900. Trethellan Smelting Works was founded by George Grenfell of Penzance in 1824, on a marshy area known as Roper's Moor, near Garras Wharf. The company prospered for several years, mostly under Williams and Harvey, who are said to have made £¼ million between 1850 and 1860. The mining slump towards the end of the century led to closure in 1890, when the building and riverside wharf was taken over by Harvey and Co. for trading purposes.

A fully laden *Queen of the Fal* of the River Fal Steamship Company steams down river to follow the meandering course of the deep-water channel to Malpas, passing that part of the eastern shore known as Sunny Corner, with Calenick Creek on the extreme left. This 1895 picture shows the first steamer of that name, built for Benney and Co. in 1893 by Cox and Co. of Falmouth. The vessel was operated mainly inside the estuary on regular river trips, although occasional excursions and charters took it out into the open sea to Gweek and as far south as Church Cove on the Lizard. A river barge stands alongside the quay, astern of the passenger tug, while on the far side of the river lower Newham Quay has been built well out of the port of Truro to handle cargoes of explosives for the mines to the west. On a narrow beach beside the Malpas road, just off the picture on the left, was the shipyard of Charles Dyer, who, after the 1860s, built several ocean-going schooners – *Pearl*, *Ulelia* and *Alpha* – for the Newfoundland trade, and *Galatea*, a brigantine. Dyer was also a ship-owner. In 1880 he built the *WJC* in which he had a third share in partnership with William Martin and John Burley. They named the 86 ton schooner using the initial of each owner's christian name. Most of Dyer's boats were for local owners, and many Truro merchants and tradesmen had shares in them. Usually manned by Truro men, they travelled afar, carrying grain from Black Sea ports, timber from Scandinavia and fruit from the Canaries.

One of the county's earliest railway lines was the West Cornwall Railway from Penzance to Truro, where the terminus was beside the river at Newham. It became redundant for passengers soon after the completion of the Cornwall railway from Plymouth to Falmouth in 1865, with its new station at the top of the town. However, it remained a goods line to the heart of the city up until the Second World War. The sign above it reads 'Great Western Railway Goods Depot'. Below, at Newham Wharf, a passenger tug is on its way up to Truro. Trading vessels lie alongside the wharf, a goods train with loaded wagons and goods sheds are in the background and the manually operated crane is at work on the quayside. The stone building behind the crane is all that is left of this once busy commercial site, now taken over by houses and offices.

This engraving shows Truro from the eastern hills of Poltisco, with the Town Quays at the junction of its two rivers, Kenwyn (left) and Allen. Apart from the essentially rural nature of the scene, with cows in the foreground and fields down almost to the Lemon Street Bridge, early maritime activity is suggested by five sailing boats and piles of timber stacked on the quay beside the lower Kenwyn.

This view dates from about 1900, when the former St Mary's church (see above) was being incorporated into the Cathedral. The town had expanded considerably. Waterside industry is indicated by several chimneys, sheds, warehouses and even larger piles of timber. On the extreme right, barely visible above the roofs of Malpas Road, is Boscawen Bridge. This was built in the mid-nineteenth century, despite protests from merchants with yards beside the River Allen above it, such as Mr Karkeek, who imported bone dust from Penryn and Exeter, and Mr Michell, who traded in lead ore, iron, coal, culm and limestone. The original bridge was replaced in the late 1860s by this handsome granite-arched bridge, which stood until the new road system was built in the 1960s.

River traffic above Malpas is determined entirely by the tide, and many vessels were too big to go farther. As a result there always has been considerable local traffic between Malpas and Truro in lighters. The tug, probably *New Resolute*, has four such shallow-draught boats in tow. These were sometimes overloaded and thus sank on the way up to Truro. The largest ships could not come above Tolverne, so timber discharged there was floated up to the saw-mills in rafts 30 ft wide. In May 1858 the *West Briton* carried an advertisement from Thomas Tregaskis of Bassett Wharf, seeking 'a steady man, as a river man, accustomed to floating rafts of timber about the Truro rivers: steady work and good wages'. The destination of the timber is shown below. The baulks of timber, enclosed by a boom, are floating offshore alongside the Malpas Road, while on Garras Wharf, opposite, is Harvey's extensive saw-mills, with the Trethellan Smelting House to the right. The Harvey business, an offshoot of the Hayle Engineering Company, opened in Truro in 1866 on Garras Wharf. The business handled coal and building materials, such as timber, cement and slate. Fire destroyed the wooden mills and sheds in 1896, and the rebuilt mills were modernized (below). Another timber firm, Fox Stanton, was taken over in 1957. The newly styled business of 'builders' merchants' in past decades has been completely transformed to embrace the ever-growing DIY market.

This view from the north of Truro and its upper river, in the late 1880s, shows the Carvedras 'fan' Viaduct, which spans the town. The railway approaches the station from the east. The new Cathedral rises above the town with its central tower blanked off until rebuilding recommenced in 1896. This was the first cathedral to be built in England since the Middle Ages. To the right are the waterside chimneys of the Trethellan Smelting Works at about the time of its closure, the gasworks and Harvey's saw-milling yard. The large Poltisco quarry is clearly visible on the left and the estuary stretches away southwards towards Malpas with Calenick Creek (centre right) and Sunny Corner (centre left). This part of the upper estuary has been completely transformed by the twentieth-century reclamation at Boscawen Park and the construction of Lighterage Quay and the associated industrial complex.

In 1890 two rival millers and grain importers at Hayle, W. Hosken and J.H. Trevithick, merged with J.S. Polkinhorn, wool stapler and agricultural seed merchant of Truro. They formed the company of Hosken, Trevithick and Polkinhorn, as the letterhead shows. In 1911 they built a new elevator and flour mill beside the river in Truro (below). In 1936 the flour milling was taken over by Spillers, but the other parts of the business associated with agriculture and gardening were carried on under the title of Farm Industries Ltd. The old name was preserved in HTP Motors, and new showrooms were built on Lemon Quay in the premises that are now Truro Pannier Market.

The engraving above, dating from the 1850s, shows the two viaducts crossing the valleys of Truro's two rivers. The prominent spire of St Mary's church is in between them. A steam train is approaching the Newham terminus of the West Cornwall Railway on the waterside, but the most outstanding feature is the width of tidal water below the town with more than twenty trading vessels alongside quays or under weigh. One large two-masted ship lies alongside Waterloo Quay in the foreground. Extensive reclamation by riverside landowners, together with severe silting, narrowed the waterway at this point, as shown in the view below of the 1890s. *New Resolute* lies alongside Back Quay where the old Custom House, closed in 1882, faces the Green. Astern of it the group of commercial buildings includes the harbour master's office, where it remains today. At the apex of the quays is the warehouse of the agricultural merchant, J. Edwards, alongside which lie three estuary barges.

Of the many events to have transformed the Truro port waterfront, the most noticeable took place in the 1920s on the lower Kenwyn. At one time the lowest crossing was at West Bridge, on the site of the present Victoria Square, with the Kenwyn flowing down what is now River Street. However, the lowest bridge has moved to Lemon Street (above), with Back Quay on the right, an estuary barge alongside. The view below, looking in the opposite direction at high tide, shows Lemon Quay (right), which, it appears from the collection of horsedrawn vehicles, was used for parking even in these early days. Commercial premises line the river on both sides, including the family drapers of N. Gill and Son on Back Quay (left) and John Julian on Lemon Quay. Julian first established himself in 1836, as a cabinet maker and upholsterer, but he is described in *Kelly's Directory* of 1893 as a 'builder, contractor, decorator, plasterer, paper-hanger, plumber, mason and turner'. The whole scene is overlooked from the hilltop by what the postcard calls the 'Wesleyan College', which was opened as a boys' boarding school in 1880.

The demands made on town centres by the increasing number of motor vehicles affected Truro in the early 1920s, when space for parking was becoming essential. As in many former ports with superfluous harbour space, the lower, formerly tidal, section of the Kenwyn River was selected for development. These two views, looking in opposite directions, show the early stages of this infilling operation. Town Quay (above), in the distance on the left, was the scene of what the *Penryn Advertiser* described as a 'singular accident' in the early days of the building of the Cathedral. The article went on to say that 'Since the new Cathedral has been commenced a large amount of earth and rubbish has been carted daily to the Town Quay to be taken away as vessels' ballast. A large heap has been accumulated on the Quay. It slants towards the edge of the river. On Friday a carrier, Mr Robins, of Shortlanesend, attempting to back his own horse and cart on the top of the pile for the purpose of setting down his load in the most convenient place, precipitated the horse and cart into the river. The tide being in, the horse was drowned. Soon afterwards the horse and cart were hauled up by the crane on the Quay. We hear that Mr Robins had insured the animal in its full value.'

These pictures show the infilling of the lower Kenwyn, nearing completion, in the mid-1930s. The rear of City Hall is prominent in both views. Beneath the present car park the Kenwyn River continues to flow, and at low tide its waters may be seen pouring out on to the mud. When parking a car or walking through this part of the city today it is interesting to contemplate the fact that within the last hundred years coastal schooners have discharged cargoes of coal, wheat and fertilizer here, and that the adjacent buildings housed such concerns as the Atlas Soap and Candle Company, the County Coach Factory, the chemical manure manufacturer, William Hale, the lime burner, Job and Son and the Truro Gas Company. As long ago as February 1888, the *West Briton* nostalgically recorded: 'None but our older readers will remember that just opposite the yard occupied by Messrs Clemens as a lime yard many vessels were formerly built and launched. The writer remembers perfectly well when a schooner and two sloops were built in the yard in question . . . For many years they traded to and from Truro to Welsh and other ports. Vessels used also to be built and launched from Trethellan yard, a little lower down the river.'

At the point where the River Allen meets the head of the estuary it splits into two channels, around what has become known as Furniss Island (see p. 156). The view upstream (above) shows considerable congestion at low tide, with two large topsail schooners and a barge alongside Trafalgar Wharf. This is better known today as Phoenix Wharf, the home of BBC Radio Cornwall. To the left is Worth's Quay, with the distinctive shelter, built in 1911 as the main passenger terminal and removed only when this whole area was changed beyond recognition with the construction of the new bypass road in the 1960s. The somewhat earlier picture (below) shows a schooner aground at the warehouse of Trounson, a corn and flour merchant, with a line of other commercial buildings in the background.

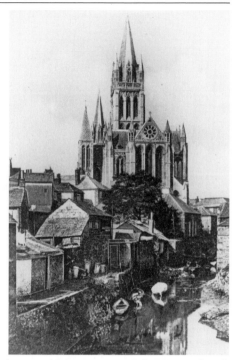

Farther up the River Allen, and formerly close to tidal water, stood St Mary's church with its distinctive spire. Consecrated as a chapel in 1259 by Bishop Bronescombe, the church was built in the early sixteenth century, but the steeple was added in 1765 to replace what had been described as 'a pitifull thing . . . like a pidgeon hut'. When it was decided to build the Cathedral, with great skill the architect, J.L. Pearson, incorporated much of the old structure into the new building. Today that part is known as St Mary's Aisle, and is regarded as Truro's parish church. Other demolition was summed up in a newspaper report of April 1880: 'The work of demolishing the old buildings, preparatory to laying the foundation stones on May 20th, has now commenced: Mill Lane is already stopped up and a portion of the Bear Inn has been taken down. The materials of 14 houses are to be sold by auction in the course of a few days'. The up-river view (right) shows the Cathedral towering over the older buildings alongside the tidal River Allen. The lowest bridge across the river has moved steadily downstream from Old Bridge Street to New Bridge Street, then to Boscawen Bridge and on to the present crossings on the new road.

This high-tide view (above) shows *New Resolute* alongside Town Quay in the early years of the twentieth century. The adjacent building displays the sign of 'J. Edwards and Sons, Seed, Manure and Implement Merchants: Wool buyers and Forage dealers', illustrating the sometimes overlooked significance of Truro as an agricultural centre. The city imported farm requirements and exported produce. At the time of this picture, however, competition from the railway had begun to make a considerable inroad into the city's maritime trade. The more comprehensive view (below), looking over Worth's Quay to Town Quay, shows a large, three-masted topsail schooner alongside the same warehouse, with *Queen of the Fal* astern. Trounson's warehouse is on the left.

The famous topsail schooner, *Mary Barrow*, with the distinctive decoration beneath the bowsprit, is unloading (probably coal) into a horsedrawn cart on the quayside. Reputedly one of the best-looking traders to visit the Fal, *Mary Barrow* was built by William Henry Lean at his yard on the Bar at Falmouth in 1891. The vessel's trading life began with trips to Newfoundland and South America, but later it was used for coastal trade, usually carrying coal, which it landed at many ports in the south-west. One of the ship's skippers was 'Mad' Captain Peter Mortensen, who became something of a legend in Cornwall for the eccentricity of his behaviour. At the far end of the line of warehouses that border the river bank is the HTP elevator (see p. 144), and on the hill above stands the former Wesleyan College.

These pictures show what was once a common sight in the port of Truro – trading vessels alongside the commercial quays. The ketch *Winifred* of Plymouth (right) is unloading (probably grain) into one of the elevators along the Malpas Road in September 1932. The topsail schooner *Lizzie* (below) and, astern, the ketch *Industry* are moored at Town Quay in the early 1900s. Such placid views of Truro give no idea of some of the more unusual events that have occurred, such as the tidal wave that swept up river in January 1880. Also, as the *West Briton* reported a year later, 'On Saturday morning the inhabitants of Truro saw a strange sight – the Truro river frozen over, from one side to another with comparatively thick ice, through which barges could not make their way, the ice extending from the rear of the market house . . . all the way down to Malpas. During the morning one of the Truro Shipping Company's vessels was taken in tow . . . by a steamer but the ice had first to be broken with crowbars by men in a boat in order to clear the way.'

Pleasure boats on the estuary came up to Truro when the tide was sufficiently high. In the absence of comparable road transport, this was the best way to travel. At low tide, as the posters advertising these journeys announced: 'a wagonette is on hand to convey passengers from Malpas to Truro'. The *Princess Victoria* (above) of the River Fal Steamship Company is reaching the end of its journey as it passes the Malpas Road warehouses, with what appears to be a full load of passengers. The passenger vessel is towing a manned rowing-boat. The reason for this is not clear: most probably the man in the boat is on hand to take a tow-rope should the larger vessel go aground. *New Resolute* (below), of the same company, is steaming down river past Trennick Row, on Truro's southern outskirts. In addition to the usual small boat a barge is also in tow. This practice, although frowned upon, was quite common.

Princess Victoria is seen here probably in 1908, early on in its career of plying between Falmouth and Truro. Built by Cox and Co. in Falmouth, this passenger tug remained in service until 1942, when it was requisitioned for war service on the Clyde. The vessel has just left the Truro quay and is passing what appears to be a recently built wall along Garras Wharf, with Town Quay in the background and a schooner alongside. The Cathedral towers over the city, with its central spire in place but awaiting the erection of the western towers to complete its imposing structure. Two passenger boats (below), identified by Alan Kittridge in his excellent book *Passenger Steamers of the River Fal* as *New Resolute* and *Queen of the Fal*, are loading at Worth's Quay. The passengers are Wesleyans on an outing in 1908. Trounson's warehouse is on the extreme right, and the adjoining sheds along Trafalgar Wharf line the River Allen behind the passenger boats.

This picture shows the north side of the Cathedral with choir and transepts beautifully reflected in the mill-pool in 1887, the year in which the Cathedral was consecrated in a 4 hour service attended by Edward, Prince of Wales and Duke of Cornwall, who had laid the foundation stone seven years before. Building on the central tower, here seen blanked off, was recommenced in 1896 and completed to its full height of 244 ft in 1905. In 1903 George, the new Prince of Wales, made the third royal visit to the Cathedral to consecrate the nave, and on the last day of this five-day visit the royal party travelled down river from Tregothnan to Falmouth, where the prince laid the foundation stone of what was named Prince of Wales Pier before returning to London by train. The 130 ft southern bell tower, the top of which is just visible over the centre of the building, above, is clad in Cornish copper which has weathered over the years to a mellow green. It was originally planned that all the roofs should be coppered but this proved too expensive.

Among the several factors that have contributed to the demise of inland ports such as Truro, the two that are most responsible are the shallowing of the water as a result of silting and the increasing use of road transport after 1920. This picture illustrates well the first factor as much as a walk at low tide along the attractive riverside paths, recently built by the local authorities as part of the Truro waterfront regeneration. The problem is not a recent one, however. In 1710 the borough authorities agreed to 'cleanse the channel'. There were plenty of good ideas, but they were all very costly and only short-term. Proposals such as straightening the channel by dredging, and building locks to hold the water at the wharves, were examined, then quietly forgotten. Mines such as Wheal Jane, which was clogging up Calenick Creek, was also responsible for obstructing the main stream, but the owners were not concerned about solving the problem. Attempts to use the mud for making bricks failed when the bricks disintegrated after firing. The rich merchants of the town – Enys, Daniell and Lemon – built quays on reclaimed mud, thus narrowing the river, and created timber ponds, which encouraged more silting, but borough complaints appeared to fall on deaf ears. In August 1873 the *West Briton*, interested as much in the health of the people as in maintaining a navigable river, reported: 'We have noticed with extreme regret for many months past, even during the very hot weather in June and July, that the sluice at Lemon Street bridge was never once used. We feel assured that if this were properly attended to the health and comfort of the inhabitants . . . would be much benefited and enhanced. It should be remembered that the Lemon bridge sluice is capable of damming back about 350,000 gallons of water twice a day and the sluice near Victoria Place 170,000 gallons. If these two sluices are let go at proper stages of the tide, seven or eight times every week, the bed of the river would be scoured and cleaned to a very great extent. Why also should not arrangements be made for scouring the eastern channel by the river Allen? The water is dammed back at Mr Orchard's mills and surely that gentleman, himself an active member of the Town Council, would offer every facility in his power for promoting the health of the town.'

The days when a scene such as this was possible at the Truro wharves are gone for ever. Three coasting vessels have reached the heart of the city and lie on the mud at low tide, probably in the late 1950s. Today, if such ships had a cargo for Truro, they would discharge it at Lighterage Quay, downstream at Newham, near the mouth of Calenick Creek. The large square building (centre) has replaced the warehouse of Edwards and Sons (see p. 151). It was built for Coast Lines and was used for storing general cargo brought up from large coasters at Falmouth by lighter. Later it was taken over by W. Penrose and Son as a showroom for camping equipment. At this point on the upper estuary the transformation has not only been the result of silting: the 'development' of Truro has involved extensive new road building across this part of the city, together with a complete reorganization of the wharves on the left, all the way down to Newham. Never again will anything but pleasure boats and small craft reach this once-thriving commercial area.

Attempts to keep the port of Truro open to large vessels were vital if supplies of coal, especially for the gasworks, and timber for Harvey's saw-mill were to arrive by sea. The dredger *Tolverne*, with an eight-man crew, was bought in 1929. It kept the channel deep enough for 600 ton colliers to reach Gas Quay until the gasworks moved to Newham in 1955. By this time trade was declining and the cost of keeping the dredger at work was too high, so it was replaced by the smaller vessel, *Reclaim*. Above, mud is being removed from the river bed off Town Quay, on which the rectangular Coast Lines warehouse dwarfs the neighbouring harbour master's office. Below, *Reclaim* has carried its load down river and is dumping the mud near the entrance to Calenick Creek, where land was being reclaimed.

Acknowledgements

However well you think you know an area, there are always people who know more. I have been fortunate to have had access to the knowledge – spoken and written – of many helpful friends. For their information, advice and loan of photographs I am most grateful. They are: Viv and Bob Acton, David Bennett-Webb, Andy Brigden, Justin Brooke, Glenys Coe, Pam Harvey, Martin Heard, George Hearle, George Hogg, Alan Kittridge, Mr and Mrs Moor, Peter Newman, Bob Paterson, Roger Penhallurick, Eileen Prout and the Mylor Darby and Joan Club, Gloria Townsend-Parker and Joan West.

Many books, newspapers and articles have been consulted, chief among which are:

Barham, Fisher, *The Creation of a Cathedral.*
Barton, D.B., *The History of Tin Mining and Smelting in Cornwall.*
Barton, D.B., *The Redruth and Chasewater Railway.*
Champion, L.D. and Simmons-Hodge, V.H., *The King Harry Steam Ferry Company Limited.*
Douch, H.L., *The Book of Truro.*
Edwards, Miss Ivy, *The Family at Rose Villa.*
Newsletters of the Restronguet Creek Society.
Olivey, Hugh P., *Notes on the Parish of Mylor.*
Publications of the Fal History Group.
Simpson, Barry, *Mining History in Restronguet Creek.*
Smith, John, *The Kennal Vale Gunpowder Company.*
Tresillian Residents' Association Magazine.
Truro Buildings Research Group, *In and Around St Clement Churchtown.*
Many editions of the *Falmouth Packet*, *West Briton* and *Western Morning News.*

My wife has continued to endure even more untidiness about the house on condition that this is my last book . . . which it is! The two Simons – Thraves and Fletcher – have put up with my problems, enquiries and bad typing with great equanimity. They and other staff at Alan Sutton Publishing have produced three books of which they and I can be pleased and proud.

To conclude this trilogy on what to me is the most beautiful part of this county, I repeat what I wrote at the end of the first volume: I hope that this may persuade some of my townsfolk to delve into drawers and boxes, to search in attics and trunks, to blow the dust from long-forgotten albums and to share their pictures and knowledge.